20TH-CENTURY COMPOSERS

American Pioneers:
Ives to Cage and Beyond

American Pioneers:
Ives to Cage and Beyond

by Alan Rich

Φ

For Betty, Judith and Nicolas

Phaidon Press Limited
Regent's Wharf
All Saints Street
London N1 9PA

Phaidon Press Inc.
180 Varick Street
New York, NY 10014

www.phaidon.com

First published 1995
Reprinted 2008
© 1995 Phaidon Press Limited

ISBN 978 0 7148 4769 6

A CIP catalogue record for this book is
available from the British Library

Cover illustration by Jean-Jacques Sempé
Designed by HDR Design
Printed in Singapore

Frontispiece, composer
Harry Partch seated among
several of the instruments
he invented to perform his
pioneering music, 1972.

Contents

Preface

The very word 'pioneer' suggests far horizons peculiarly American. The founders of cities in the hills and plains of France, in the Rhine valley and the Italian seacoast, are lost in the swirl of ancient lore. But the wagon trains that carried America's explorers and settlers from the comfortable cities of the East Coast, westward through unknown lands to the shadow of the Rockies and beyond to the Pacific shore, are a part of modern history. America has cherished its pioneers. Their descendants are with us still.

There was more to be explored by these first generations of pioneers than the beckoning territory. America's creative artists, too, were no less obsessed with staking new claims in unfamiliar worlds than were their compatriots. The struggles of a new nation to assert its individuality – to burst through the confines of traditional modes of expression, to forge new modes that reflected their own take on their hard-won American environment – shaped the novels of James Fenimore Cooper, the defiant essays of Henry Thoreau, the exultant if sometimes heartbroken lyrics of Walt Whitman, the adoring mountainscapes of the Hudson River painters.

Music, being the most mysterious of the expressive arts, bred its American pioneers relatively late. The patrons of the great performing institutions, the symphony orchestras and the opera associations, were content at first to model their establishments along European lines. American readers thrilling to the exploits of Fenimore Cooper's leather-stockinged explorers were, at the same time, confining their musical explorations to the imported works of Handel and Beethoven. Rather than staking out claims on their own soil, America's first serious composers learned to copy their European forebears. Not until the late nineteenth and early twentieth century did it occur to an American composer that there was pioneering work to be done on native turf, that America itself offered the kind of indigenous richness of folk melody and dance that had fuelled the music of Weber, Dvořák and Smetana, of Grieg, Tchaikovsky and Verdi, in the regions where classical music had been born.

The American musical pioneers found many ways to invent their new kinds of serious music. The breadth of a continent separated the convoluted, defiant clangour of a Charles Ives tone poem from the sensuous Orientalisms in the percussion and prepared-piano works of Henry Cowell and his protégés John Cage and Lou Harrison. On opposite coasts, Edgard Varèse and Harry Partch developed their individual ways to free music from the tyranny of a mere twelve notes to the octave; generations later, in electronic workshops in New York and San Francisco, the expanded ranks of the composer–electricians strove even more ardently toward the same goal.

Great upheavals in artistic expression always seem to surface from a welter of underbrush. The first operas, composed in Italy around 1600, were poky affairs; then Claudio Monteverdi demonstrated the expressive power in the new medium. The first generation of Classical composers, the sons of J. S. Bach and their cohorts, denied their stylistic paternity and produced reams of merely correct, bland music; then came Haydn and Mozart. It does not always follow, in any field where pioneers have worked, that the ground-breaking creations are necessarily the masterworks in their genre. America's musical pioneers were prolific, for the most part; the catalogues of the works of Ives, Cowell, Harrison and Cage are voluminous affairs, studded with the occasional masterpiece but filled in as well with lesser works of mere historic interest. Edgard Varèse, on the other hand, produced no more than a dozen works that establish his place among the pioneers; he emphatically disinherited most of what he composed before moving to the USA. Colin McPhee, enormously influential for his pioneering researches into the music of Indonesia, actually com- posed only one major work that embodies his theories of musical transculturation. Yet that one work cast a huge shadow over the thinking of further generations.

The pioneers, therefore, are not always the ones who make their new-found land explode into full bloom. Even so, a short list of masterpieces from the hands of America's musical pioneers may serve as glowing testimony to the strength, spirit and imagination of their creators: the 'Concord' Sonata and Fourth Symphony of Ives; Varèse's *Amériques* and *Arcana*; any one (or a dozen) of Cowell's pre-1920 piano pieces; the *Song Books* and *Music for 17* of Cage; Harrison's Piano Concerto and *Lo Koro Sutro*; Partch's *Revelation in the Courthouse Park*.

The way of the pioneers is made smooth by the brave souls who love their spirit (and sometimes, if not necessarily always, their music). Three neighbours of mine fight the good fight with uncommon nobility. Two of them open their homes to composers and invite in small, supportive audience groups; they give over much of their time to hunting down new music and making it known. Sixty years ago the third braved public outcry, fearlessly leading world premières of many works central to this survey. To them – Betty Freeman, Judith Rosen and Nicolas Slonimsky – this book is dedicated.

Alan Rich
Los Angeles, 1995

I

The rough-cut contrasts in
Missouri-born Thomas Hart
Benton's *The Pathfinder*
captured the romantic vision
of the American pioneer.

... the pioneer's courage: his desire to hack
a way through the forest since he has, indeed,
no alternative

Wilfrid Mellers,
Music in a New Found Land, 1964

Prelude

Music arrived early in the New World, in the hearts and minds of its first settlers. The religious fervour that drove the colonists westward across the fearsome Atlantic found its stern and uncompromising voice in music as well as in preaching. Like the fierce winters that buffeted the Puritan pioneers in the Massachusetts Bay Colony, the first printed American music – the *Bay Psalm Book* of 1640 which provided metrical versions of the Psalms to be sung to 'very neere fourty common tunes as they are collected out of our chief musicians' – was an austere affair.

Little evidence exists to suggest that the first generations of American settlers had much awareness of the musical marvels they had left behind in the homeland: the operas of Monteverdi and Scarlatti, the grandiose anthems and theatre music of John Blow and Henry Purcell. There is nothing to tell us what hymns and motets stirred the crowd's frenzies as witches were hunted down and tortured in Salem late in the seventeenth century. To the north, the Jesuits from France had brought a far more extensive musical treasure to their outposts in Eastern Canada; such were the battle lines between English and French that very little of this music travelled southward. To the south, similarly, the ranks of the Spanish conquerors included both priests and musicians, who countenanced the mingling of their traditional European liturgy with the lavish heritage of Mayan and Incan musical ritual. None of this extensive legacy, however, seems to have travelled northward in its own time; it is only recently, in fact, that a vast repertory of Latin-American chant and polyphony has been unearthed, studied and recorded.

By the mid-eighteenth century, however, America's new urban society was ready to deal with the gentler of life's amenities. New York City's first pipe organ was installed in the Dutch Reformed Church in 1724. The city's first public concert took place in 1736, in a vintner's house next to the historic (and still-standing) Fraunces' Tavern: this was a programme of songs and chamber music organized by the

The *Bay Psalm Book*, printed in 1640 for the church-goers of the Massachusetts Bay Colony, was the first music published in North America.

THE
VVHOLE
BOOKE OF PSALMES
Faithfully
TRANSLATED *into* ENGLISH
Metre.

Whereunto is prefixed a difcourfe de-
claring not only the lawfullnes, but alfo
the neceffity of the heavenly Ordinance
of finging Scripture Pfalmes in
the Churches of
God.

Coll. III.

*Let the word of God dwell plenteoufly in
you, in all wifdome, teaching and exhort-
ing one another in Pfalmes, Himnes, and
fpirituall Songs, finging to the Lord with
grace in your hearts.*

Iames V.

*If any be afflicted, let him pray, and if
any be merry let him fing pfalmes.*

Imprinted
1640

German-born organist Carl Theodor Pachelbel, son of the renowned Johann. By the 1770s New York audiences had been vouchsafed regular access to the music of Handel (including large chunks of *Messiah*); in the 1780s the music of Haydn had also made its entry into New York's burgeoning concert life, with Boston and Philadelphia not far behind.

America's growth in expanse and prosperity in the nineteenth century was accompanied by a crescendo of musical activity. On Christmas Eve 1815, proper Bostonians flocked to the inaugural concert of the Handel and Haydn Society, where a chorus of ninety men and ten women sang selections from both namesake composers; that cultural monument, too, still exists. After several insignificant

King's (later Stone)
Chapel, Boston, which
housed the birth of
American Unitarianism in
1783, was also famed
for its musical excellence,
as it is to this day.

failed attempts, grand opera gained its first substantial toehold at
New York's Park Theatre in 1825; among the sponsors was none other
than Lorenzo da Ponte, formerly the librettist of Mozart's finest
operas and now an established operatic producer and teacher of
Italian literature in New York. Visiting orchestras from Europe seren-
aded audiences in most major East Coast cities with symphonies and
concertos by Haydn, several of Johann Sebastian Bach's sons (still at
that time more popular than their father) and Beethoven. By
1842 New York was ready for a permanent orchestra of its own, the
still flourishing New York Philharmonic.

European concert and operatic life had been nurtured for the most
part by governmental subsidy. Major cities supported their orchestras
and theatres out of municipal funds; Richard Wagner's music dramas
thrived under the patronage of Bavaria's Ludwig II. Nineteenth-
century America had no such benevolent governmental sponsorship;
not until recent times, in fact, has there been the means for chan-
nelling Federal funds to the arts. The American 'aristocracy' was its
private corporate leadership. A single individual, the millionaire
stockbroker Henry Lee Higginson, financed the founding of the
Boston Symphony Orchestra in 1881, built its splendid concert hall,

New York's Carnegie Hall
was inaugurated in 1891,
despite fears that it might
be too far 'uptown' to
attract crowds. Those fears
have long proved
unfounded.

Above, in 1882, two years
after its founding, the Boston
Symphony sat for this portrait
on the ornate stage of its
Music Hall, which was
replaced by Symphony Hall
in 1900. Major Henry Lee
Higginson, *right,* founded the
orchestra at his own expense,
and remained its sole patron
for its first forty years.

and remained the sole owner and musical arbiter for the orchestra's first four decades. American steel bankrolled New York's Carnegie Hall; American railroads maintained New York's opera, and when, around 1880, the choice box seats in the Academy of Music began to be bought up by the new money of recent immigrants, to the horror of the ruling 'old-money' Vanderbilt family, the Vanderbilts simply built a new opera house with tighter control and fewer boxes.

If the railroad-baron Vanderbilts typified America's obsession with maintaining control over a 'pure' indigenous cultural life, just the opposite seemed to apply to attitudes concerning the development of a native American serious music. In other fields of artistic endeavour Americans worked hard to develop an individualistic language, to cut the ties that bound them to a European ancestry. The painter Edward Hicks, the novelist and essayist Washington Irving, New England's Transcendentalists (who translated the initial inspiration of the German philosopher Immanuel Kant into a resolutely American outlook) shared an obsession to create a native artistic language. Henry David Thoreau (1817–62), most revolutionary of the Transcendentalists, most defiant in his revolt against the demands of society and government, was to serve as icon, decades after his death, to generations of America's pioneer composers.

In Thoreau's own time, however, an ambitious American composer seeking fame and fortune knew that there was no pathway to success except through a thorough and laborious annealing of musical style in the crucibles of the European conservatories. There were exceptions, of course. George Frederick Bristow (1825–98), violinist and composer, had what might pass as an American musical upbringing, except that his father, his principal teacher, had emigrated from England to New York only a year before his son's birth. To the younger Bristow's credit, however, let it be noted that for several months in 1854 he abandoned his post in the New York Philharmonic's string section in a one-man strike to protest at the orchestra's neglect of American music in favour of the works of foreigners.

By the time of Bristow's demonstration, America had already assimilated a fair amount of the worldwide repertory. Handel, Haydn, Mozart, Beethoven, Mendelssohn and Schumann were by then household names; J. S. Bach's music, some of it in atrocious Romantic

Nineteenth-century American writers and artists, native and adopted, delighted in the landscape in its infinite variety. This 1830 view of New York's Sawkill Falls, *opposite*, was included in William Cullen Bryant's famous collection of engravings entitled *The American Landscape*.

Thomas Hart Benton's
Women's Place and the Old-
Time Doctor and the Grange
is a panorama of small-town
activity in turn-of-the-century
America, with a feminist
orator haranguing the crowd
on the left and a country
doctor in action on the right.

Henry Thoreau's *Walden, or Life in the Woods* (its 1854 engraved title-page shown *below*) defined the freedom of spirit that was to motivate such later pioneers as John Cage. *Right,* Thoreau is seen in an early portrait, still functioning as a well-dressed, law-abiding citizen of Concord, Massachusetts.

THOREAU.

Below, the woods near
Thoreau's Walden Pond, in
eastern Massachusetts about
twenty miles north of Boston,
are still well protected
from the encroachments
of developers.
Right, after Thoreau,
no-one better epitomized
the American rugged
individualist than the poet
and essayist Walt Whitman.

re-orchestrations, had begun to make its way, both in Europe and
America. An extraordinary Boston publication, *Dwight's Journal of
Music* (1852–81), kept its weekly readers aware of contemporary trends
and composers throughout the musical world, dealing at considerable
length with the rising star of Richard Wagner, and greeting with
wary enthusiasm such novelties as the 'difficult, strange, wild,
ultra modern' First Piano Concerto of 'the young professor' Peter
Tchaikovsky (which actually had its world première in Boston).

By 1900 there were major orchestras, firmly established and
offering continuous concert schedules year after year, in New York,
Boston, Chicago, Cincinnati, St Louis and Pittsburgh. Philadelphia
joined the list in 1900, Minneapolis three years later. Several
of those cities maintained opera companies as well; with a little

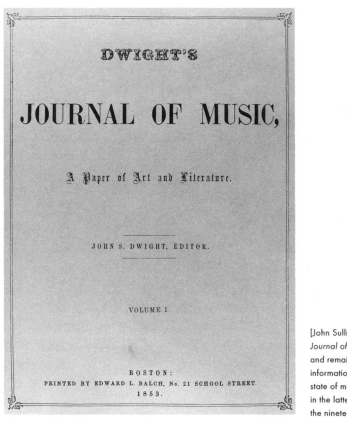

[John Sullivan] *Dwight's
Journal of Music* was,
and remains, a trove of
information about the
state of music in America
in the latter half of
the nineteenth century.

Right, Theodore Thomas conducting an orchestra in New York's Steinway Hall in 1890. Conductor, orchestra builder and tireless advocate for the best in music, Thomas, *below,* went on from a successful conductor's career in New York to found the Chicago Symphony Orchestra.

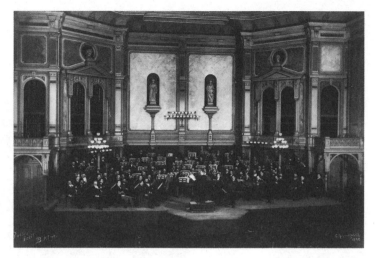

Baltimore's Peabody Conservatory was founded in 1857, making it America's first music school.

METROPOLITAN OPERA HOUSE
Broadway & 39th St.
copyright 1912 By
IRVING UNDERHILL, N.Y.
B19204

Inaugurated in 1883 and forsaken for a newer venue in 1966, New York's Metropolitan Opera House was always regarded as America's most prestigious operatic stage.

imagination and a lot of patience you can make out the sounds of performances at the Metropolitan Opera House in New York from before 1900, recorded on cylinders on primitive equipment backstage in the house and now reissued on digitally re-edited versions.

American composer, foreign composer: it was not easy to distin- guish between them in the latter decades of the nineteenth century; American audiences approached all new music with caution (a situation not greatly changed today). The growing nation offered its prospective musicians a fair amount of music training at home; the first American college-level music department had opened at Oberlin, in Ohio, as early as 1837; Boston, Cincinnati, Chicago and Baltimore followed suit soon after. Still the European stamp of approval in an American composer's credentials did serve as some guarantee of respectability that native resources might not easily have matched. Even the flamboyant Louis Moreau Gottschalk (1829–69), who wrote enormously popular piano pieces incorporating tunes and rhythms from his native Louisiana, had found it advisable to study abroad – in Paris, where both Hector Berlioz and Frédéric Chopin took note of his talents. Most Americans – among them John Knowles Paine (1839–1906), Edward MacDowell (1860–1908) and Horatio Parker (1863–1919) – found study in Germany more congenial. MacDowell, in fact, won the admiration of Franz Liszt, held a teaching post at a prestigious German academy for several years and had some of his music published by the illustrious firm of Breitkopf & Härtel, whose previous clients had included Ludwig van Beethoven. These were the composers, their style so Europeanized as to pass quite readily as the latest attentive followers of Liszt, Schumann or Brahms, who best fulfilled America's idea of a 'native' composer at the end of the nineteenth century.

As decisively as the American militants had won their political freedom in 1776, America's pioneer composers set out, starting around 1900, to earn their musical freedom, to create an indigenous American music distinguishable from the European sonatas and symphonies that had, until then, served as role models. What, then, defined the 'pioneer spirit' that was to play a major role in the shaping of the new American musical language, starting right at the beginning of the twentieth century? Above all, it was the assertion by ensuing generations of American composers that the old European

models no longer represented the inevitable pathways for all time. As
the Pilgrims and Puritans had cut their ties with Europe in sailing to
unknown lands in the seventeenth century, as the settlers in following
decades turned their backs on the urban comforts of the big cities and
pushed their way westward in covered wagons and on horseback to
discover the fullness of the American continent, so America's pioneer
composers determined to seek out new sources and new structures for
their artistic inspiration.

No longer tied to the rubrics implied in the music of the European
masters, they sought inspiration in musical sources hitherto unexplored. For Charles Ives, whose father George had instilled in him a
passion for experimentation, the music of American brass bands and
the rough-cut hymn-singing of American revivalist meetings served
as rich new source material. Henry Cowell's inspiration stemmed
from a lifelong obsession to invent new and original sounds. For John
Cage, another inventor of sounds, inspiration came from both the
music and the spirituality of the Orient, as it also did for Cage's
friend and disciple Lou Harrison. Their enthusiasm for inventing

Not all music was on formal
indoor stages. This view of
the Boston Brass Band comes
from an 1851 edition of
*Gleason's Pictorial Drawing
Room Companion.*

Acting on celestial
instruction to lead the
Mormon people westward,
Joseph Smith and his
successor Brigham Young
crossed almost the entire
continent, eventually settling
in Salt Lake City, Utah.
This engraving depicts a
moment along the way,
an encampment in Illinois
in 1858.

new sounds drew its heat from their pioneering obsessions, and also
from the fact that performers on traditional instruments – soloists
and full symphony orchestras – were notoriously timid about playing
new music. So Cowell, Cage and Harrison raided junkyards and
assembled pioneering 'orchestras' out of resonant brake drums and
truck springs and metal thunder sheets; composers in later generations explored farther horizons with sounds electronically produced
and manipulated. Once considered a primitive and impoverished
relative at the cultural banquet, America's innovative composers
became the role models throughout our century for musical dissidents
the world over.

In 1900 the 26-year-old Charles Edward Ives was in his second
year as a well-paid employee of an insurance company. In his free
time, he presided over the organ loft at New York's Central
Presbyterian Church, where he occasionally tried out some of his
own compositions on the captive congregation, including unconventional re-harmonizations of familiar old hymns and organ
improvisations that could sometimes take headlong flight well away
from any stable tonality. On one occasion, he later remembered,
the pastor 'turned around and glowered'. With that glower, delivered
at the advent of the new century, the day of America's musical
pioneers had dawned.

2

Mahantango Valley Farm,
window-shade painting by
an unknown American
primitive, late nineteenth-
century, from the National
Gallery of Art, Washington

*Maybe music was not intended to satisfy the
curious definiteness of man. Maybe it is better to
hope that music will always be a transcendental
language in the most extravagant sense.*

Charles Ives,
Essays Before a Sonata, 1920

Charles Ives

In the spring of 1947 the judges of the Columbia University Pulitzer
Prizes, given annually in the fields of journalism and the arts, awarded
the music prize to a work composed forty-three years before but
only performed for the first time in the previous year. The composer,
Charles Edward Ives, was then seventy-three and in poor health. In
1904, when he composed his Third Symphony, he was out to conquer
the world. In 1947, however, he had not composed a note of music in
twenty-five years; aside from a few out-of-the-way concerts in obscure
halls, little of his extraordinary legacy of music had yet been heard.
When the pianist John Kirkpatrick gave the première of Ives's second
sonata, the 'Concord', the *New York Herald-Tribune* critic Lawrence
Gilman described it as 'the greatest music composed by an American,
and the most deeply and essentially American in impulse and impli-
cation'. That happened in 1939, at a sparsely attended Town Hall
recital. Gilman was the only critic in the audience; the august *New
York Times* had not seen fit to attend. Charles Ives's time had not yet
come. A small but ardent group of supporters kept his name alive,
most of them composers whose own creative methods – indeed, their
way of regarding the entire phenomenon of music – had been
changed by their association with Ives.

The Pulitzer Prize, the American equivalent of the stamp of
approval accorded a cut of beef found to be free of taint, opened the
floodgates. For the last seven years of his life, Charles Ives was to
reap the adulation the world had long owed him. Old and enfeebled,
nearly blind, he greeted the Pulitzer judges with an attempt at
something like his old gruffness. 'Prizes are the badges of mediocrity',
he huffed, and gave away the $500 prize money to another composer,
John Becker, whom Ives judged to be more in need than himself.
Secretly, however, he revelled in the world's rediscovery of his music,
even to the point, in 1951, of abandoning his long-standing aversion
to hearing music on the radio. He listened as Leonard Bernstein and
the New York Philharmonic gave the world première, forty-nine years

late, of an even earlier work, his Second Symphony of 1902; he even invoked the composer's prerogative, letting Bernstein know in no uncertain terms that the tempos had been too slow. The work had gathered dust for nearly half a century, but Ives had preserved his own image of his Second Symphony and knew how it was meant to sound.

At home in the unremarkable industrial town of Danbury, Connecticut, and later at Yale University, Charles Ives had had ample chance to absorb the pioneer spirit in full measure. His father, George Ives, had at the tender age of seventeen been the bandmaster of the First Connecticut Heavy Artillery during the American Civil War; no less a music critic than General Ulysses S. Grant had mentioned to

George Ives, Charles' father, at the age of forty-five (1890). As a bandmaster in the American Civil War, he had won the admiration of General U.S. Grant.

President Abraham Lincoln that Ives's band was 'the best in the Army'. At the war's end George Ives returned to Danbury, founded a local brass band, led the choir at Danbury's Baptist Church, taught music in several schools, and in January 1874 married Mary Parmelee, daughter of the town's leading church soloist. Charles Edward Ives, older of George Ives's two sons, was born the following October.

He had his first musical training from his father, being present at George's band rehearsals almost from the time he could walk. At home his musical horizons were further expanded, as family and friends frequently gathered for nights of chamber-music playing. Bach and Beethoven, Charles later remembered, were among the favoured composers; Haydn and Mozart were considered too easy on the ears. George gave his son formal lessons as well, in drums, cornet and piano. At thirteen, Charles composed a piece for the band, *Holiday Quickstep*; it was reviewed approvingly in the local press. 'Master Ives is certainly a musical genius', proclaimed the *Danbury Evening News* on 17 January 1888. '*Holiday Quickstep* is worthy a [*sic*] place with productions of much older heads.' By fourteen he was ensconced in the organ loft at the Danbury First Baptist Church, the youngest paid musician in the entire state of Connecticut.

From his father, Charles Ives inherited the disrespect for hide-bound musical correctitude that was to guide his career from childhood on. He remembered an occurrence from childhood, when George Ives discovered his prodigious son perched at the piano, banging away all by himself in an attempt to play both a melody and also the drum rhythms he had heard at band rehearsals. 'It's all right to do that, Charlie,' Ives remembered his father's saying, 'if you know what you're doing.' Those words were to linger long in Charles Ives's artistic conscience.

George Ives held a lifelong fascination with the notion of experimentation, spending long hours playing musical instruments across a nearby pond to study the nature of echoes, and instilling an enlightened view of music's far horizons at home as well. His favourite kind of musical hell-raising was to rattle the bones of traditional musical practice, to turn the classical precepts of harmony and rhythm upside-down. As part of his son's training, George inflicted such ear-stretching musical exercises as playing a song accompaniment in one key and obliging Charles to sing the melody in another.

Asked by another musician why, with all his musical training, he persisted in drawing so much dissonance from his long-suffering piano, George replied, 'I may have perfect pitch but thank God the piano doesn't.'

At seventeen, Charles proved himself an adept son and heir in a set of variations (for organ, but later orchestrated) on the hymn tune *America* (the same melody as 'God Save the Queen') which included among its catalogue of audacities two interludes composed in several simultaneous keys and one variation in the form of a lugubrious and disrespectful polonaise. Another of George's experiments also obviously remained fresh in Charles's mind. On a given afternoon, George Ives had arranged for his own band and another band to march around the Danbury town square in opposite directions, each playing a different piece and thereby setting up a fearsome cacophony. The Danbury citizenry was not amused; surviving reports dismissed the stunt as merely 'discordant'. But in one of Charles Ives's most daring compositional experiments, the movement from *Three Places in New England* entitled *General Putnam's Camp*, two brass bands within the full orchestra play conflicting tunes in conflicting rhythms, creating a diabolical chaos for listeners and players alike (not to mention the conductor, who must control two separate rhythmic patterns).

George Ives died suddenly, of a stroke at the age of forty-nine in late 1894, 'just at the time I needed him most', said Charles. He had left Charles 'that awful vacuum', as he later put it, but bequeathed to him also the foundation for a life to be spent in questioning, challenging and thumbing his nose at everything traditional musicians held dear. Father and son had been, over a decade, a two-man force in musical experimentation. 'One thing I am certain of,' Charles later wrote, 'that if I have done anything good in music it was ... because of my father'. Their last collaboration had been a series of psalm-settings composed by the son for the father's church choir in Danbury, with Charles fulfilling George's concept of musical anarchy by imposing on the beloved Biblical verses a whole range of unconventional musical devices – crashing dissonances and harmonic tricks designed to thwart the expectations of singers and listeners in equal measure.

Charles entered Yale University that year, primarily to continue his studies in composition; to help out with finances he got a job as organist at one of the collegiate churches. Like most other academic music departments, Yale's was dominated by the automatic assumption that serious composition could stem from only one source, the venerated techniques of the European masters. Horatio Parker had recently been appointed to head Yale's music department, bringing to his classes the light of his own knowledge of solid Teutonic counterpoint and stolid Victorian structure – which, needless to say, he

Charles Ives in his late teens, ready to storm the bastions of musical conservatism at Yale University

had acquired at the source. Ordinarily, Yale's undergraduates were denied access to music courses; through the intercession of well-placed friends and relatives of the Ives family, the young man was admitted to the sanctum.

Perceived wisdom tends to assign Parker an adversarial role *vis-à-vis* his most famous pupil: the hidebound conservative against the hot-tempered rebel. That is not quite accurate, however. The Brahmsian strain that he absorbed into his own style during his European studies was, after all, the reflection of a composer who was himself regarded as something of a modernist in his own time. 'Exit in Case of Brahms' was the sign suggested for posting in Boston's Symphony Hall by a fearful critic. Parker's choral works, and the opera *Mona*, had their quotient of daring; the influence of Debussy, as much as that of the Central Europeans, pervades his best work. No less a contemporary innovator than the formidable Roger Sessions could be numbered among his pupils.

Nevertheless, Parker's teaching was important to Ives in furthering the knowledge of music's traditional rules that he had already gained from his father. But the work he brought to class far exceeded the rubrics; it leaned more towards the spirit of experimentation that George Ives had encouraged – however cautiously – so many years before. After three or four weeks, Parker ordered his young pupil to desist from bringing 'that sort of thing' into his classroom and to stick to the regular assignments. Ives acquiesced, but merely stepped up his off-campus compositional activity, cajoling local musicians into playing his music, or trying some of it out on his church congregation.

In 1895 he began work on his most ambitious project to date, the work which ultimately emerged as his First Symphony. Not surprisingly, Horatio Parker was aghast at the first draft; it would not do, he proclaimed, for a symphony purportedly in the key of D minor to run through seven or eight other keys within the space of its first theme. Parker waxed even more furious at the 'reprehensible' ending of the work (in – horror! – a key other than the one at the start), and ordered Ives to rewrite it. This time Ives refused; a compromise was eventually struck whereby the symphony at least began and ended in the same key but wandered far and wide in between.

All told, Ives's four years at Yale form an almost classic study of
a brilliant but untameable mind in its formative stages. He was a
popular figure; he joined student fraternities and even composed
music for some of their social functions. Before Yale he had been an
accomplished athlete, but George Ives, knowing his son's propensity
for distraction, had forbidden him to go out for college sports. Even
so, Ives's overall scholastic record at Yale ranged from abysmal to
unremarkable; it would be hard to imagine the adamant Horatio
Parker lending much of a helping hand to further the career of this
young firebrand.

On his own, removed from the disapproving glare of Yale's music
faculty, the collegian Ives composed prolifically. He began work on
the First Symphony in 1897 and completed it just before graduation
in May 1898. As with the three later symphonies, the first gathered
dust, unheard for over half a century; its first performance took place
in 1953. A year before the First Symphony, Ives composed one other

An American church choir
in rehearsal, in 1871,
preparing the kind of music
Ives was to carry into his own
large-scale compositions

large-scale work, a string quartet subtitled 'A Revival Service',
dating from 1896. True to its subtitle, the quartet drew upon Ives's
memories of time in church organ lofts; among the hymn tunes
incorporated into the four-movement piece were 'From Greenland's
Icy Mountains', which became the subject of the contrapuntal first
movement and the rousing 'Stand Up, Stand Up for Jesus', which
strides through the finale and, at the end, is smashed against another
theme to create a melodic, harmonic and rhythmic clash worthy of
George Ives's brass-band escapades. The 'Greenland' movement must
have pleased Ives especially, since he later rescored it (with minimal
changes) to serve as the third movement of the Fourth Symphony.
But the quartet, too, was a long time in reaching its rightful audience.
It received its first performance, in an abridged version, in 1957.

In general, Ives accomplished far less in his formal studies at Yale
than in his extracurricular activity. 'In the music classes at Yale', he
later wrote, ' ... ideas were not so much suppressed as ignored. I got
a little fed up on too much counterpoint and classroom exercises,
maybe because, somehow, counterpoint ... became a kind of exercise
on paper instead of on the mountains.'

Free at last from scholastic trammels, Ives was obliged in 1898 to
weigh the comparative folly value of a life in music or one in the real
world. Fortunately, a family friend found him a position in New
York in the Mutual Insurance Company. He took lodgings with
several former classmates, in a mid-Manhattan apartment they called
'Poverty Flat'. At Mutual he struck up what was to become a
valuable friendship with an applications clerk named Julian Myrick,
six years Ives's junior.

The times were not propitious for launching a career in insurance,
at least with a monolithic firm such as Mutual. Outcries resounded;
charges of shady dealings, nepotism and reckless investments had
brought down the wrath of governmental investigators as well as
private victims. Ives, however, saw himself as a possible saviour, the
founder of a new firm – and, indeed, a new concept – to woo
prospective clients with promises of cleaner business practices than
the major firms could provide. The mix of Ives's visions of new
horizons for the insurance industry and Myrick's practicality suggested an ongoing partnership, which resulted some years later in the
independent agency initially called Ives & Company and, eventually,

New York in 1900 (corner of
Broadway and 38th Street,
with the Metropolitan Opera
on the left), a city ripe for
conquest by the 26-year-old
Charles Ives

017415. WILLIAMSBURG BRIDGE.

The Williamsburg Bridge, connecting the lower end of Manhattan with the Borough of Brooklyn, a vital link in the ever-expanding metropolis of New York

Ives & Myrick. A pamphlet written by Ives on estate planning, a
message of solace and advice to prospective purchasers of insurance,
is still highly regarded and often quoted in the industry today. The
company prospered; for the rest of his life it allowed Ives a level of
financial security seldom if ever attained by composers afflicted with
revolutionary ideas.

Ives was able to pursue those ideas at weekends, banging away at
his battered piano in what his 'Poverty Flat' housemates came to call
'resident disturbances'. From 1898 to 1900 he was organist at a church
in Bloomfield, New Jersey, thereafter at the Central Presbyterian
Church in Manhattan – a block from the august realm of Carnegie
Hall, whose rafters would be shaken over the next half-century by
only one work of Ives, and that only in a sight-reading workshop. At
Central Presbyterian he was able to have his music performed; an
extensive but rather tame cantata, *The Celestial Country*, was sung
there in 1902 and was amiably reviewed in the *New York Times* and
Musical Courier, the first mention of an Ives work in the metropolitan
press. As organist, Ives had the chance to inflict some of his harmonic
experiments on his congregations during his weekly improvisations;
if he wrote any of this music down, however, it has not survived.
When he resigned the church job in May 1902, he absent-mindedly
left behind whatever manuscripts he had created; they were
destroyed by a church employee during a spasm of housecleaning.

The inability to get his music performed did little to slow Ives's
creative impulses during his New York years; resigning the church job
seems to have left him with greater time and energy for composition.
He had begun a Second Symphony, more densely textured than the
first (if a few minutes shorter) while still at Yale, but worked harder
on it after graduation; it was substantially complete in mid-1902. As
a representation of the 'pure' Ives manner, this work stands tall, a
remarkable blend in which dozens of American folk and fiddle tunes,
patriotic songs and hymns standing cheek-by-jowl are stirred into a
Romantic orchestral matrix that might even earn the imprimatur
of the good grey avatar of tradition, Horatio Parker himself.

The Third Symphony followed soon afterwards, brought to completion in 1904. Smaller in scope than the two earlier symphonies,
scored for a chamber orchestra, the work gives off a calm spirituality
that seems more consistent, less likely to dart off in unexpected

directions, than Ives's previous orchestral forays. It bears the subtitle 'The Camp Meeting'; each of its three movements bears a further title: *Old Folks Gathering, Children's Day* and *Communion*. Rather than regarding its fund of hymn-tune borrowings as an incidental effect, the Third Symphony draws upon them as its principal material, fashioning a totally original contrapuntal fantasy out of found objects – 'a kind of crossway', as Ives was later to write, 'between the older ways and the newer ways'.

More and more, the 'newer ways' seem to have taken hold of the young man's spirit. In the ten years after Yale, Ives composed with furious energy; the need to discipline his time between insurance and music seemed to work to the advantage of both sides of his existence. Most of his best-known orchestral works date from this decade: evocative and descriptive pieces (*Thanksgiving Day, Runaway Horse, Over the Pavements* and a work called *From the Steeples and Mountains* composed for church bells and instrumental ensemble) that would surely have gladdened George Ives's inventor's heart, and, in partic- ular, a set that Ives called 'Two Contemplations', consisting of *The Unanswered Question* and *Central Park in the Dark*.

Both movements – heard singly or together – form a strange and wonderful fantasy. *The Unanswered Question,* is still revered for its strangeness; its mystical tone and (to listeners otherwise fearful of any music of this century) welcome brevity have made it one of the

A church camp meeting in Ives's own state of Connecticut. His Third Symphony is subtitled 'The Camp Meeting' and abounds in the kind of hymns which are probably being sung here.

best-known American works. Scored for a small ensemble, it is among
other things a remarkable anticipation of today's 'ambient', music,
in which space plays a role. String players on the stage sound soft,
gleaming chords representing, to Ives, 'the Silence of the Druids'.
Offstage, a solo trumpet propounds 'The Perennial Question of
Existence' in tuneful, hymn-like scraps, while 'flutes and other
persons' move around the stage as 'the Flying Answerers'. In *Central
Park*, for a larger ensemble, the sense of space is again invoked; the
listener seems to stand at the edge of the park while bands play off
in the distance, and the orchestra depicts the distant sounds of automobile horns and shouting newsboys – a memory, beyond doubt,
of George Ives's duelling brass bands back in Danbury – while the
orchestra envelops the scene in an undulating evocation of a dark
summer sky. Today the two 'Contemplations' are among Ives's most
familiar music, challenged only by the more daunting complexities
of *Three Places in New England*; composed in 1906, they were to wait
forty years for their first hearing.

A harmonious association:
the 73-year-old Charles
Ives (right) stands with his
one-time insurance partner
Julian Myrick.

In 1906 Ives and Myrick finalized their partnership; their new firm began life on 1 January 1907 and astounded sceptics with quick and impressive success, largely brought on by Ives's enlightened and revolutionary approach to the matter of estate planning; the partnership endured until Ives's retirement in 1930. A change was imminent in Ives's personal life as well. Since 1905 he had been courting Harmony Twichell, known as 'the most beautiful girl in Hartford', one of nine children in an illustrious family that enjoyed the friendship of such notable figures as the writer Mark Twain. Quite likely, their courtship produced the motive power for the splendid music Ives was composing at the time. They were married in June 1908.

The bridegroom was thirty-four years old. His face had grown long and narrow; his hair had grown thin – 'thinking of music', a friend suggested. His business was sound and growing. A small stroke a few years earlier had given momentary concern, and Ives had been obliged to abandon the athletic exercises he had enjoyed in younger days. The young couple moved out of 'Poverty Flat' and took lodgings further uptown in Manhattan.

In 1910 the eminent New York conductor Walter Damrosch was persuaded to examine Ives's First Symphony and to give at least one movement of the work an informal reading with his New York Symphony Orchestra. Scion of a family of conductors, organizers and dictators of taste that was to dominate New York's musical life until the 1920s, Damrosch made no secret of his contempt for 'difficult new music'. He could praise a new work for its 'workmanship' but never for what it had to say. 'Charming', Damrosch cried out – according to Ives's later remembrance – at the start of the movement. Then came fiasco; Damrosch kept stopping the orchestra to correct what he considered wrong notes; arriving at the passage where some of the players perform in multiples of two beats against others in multiples of three – a practice in which Schumann and Brahms had indulged decades earlier – Damrosch stopped the orchestra altogether. 'Young man,' he called out patronizingly, 'you'll just have to make up your mind! Do you want two or three?' As far as Damrosch was concerned, Ives decided, he wanted neither. Years later, in a burst of aimless self-destruction, he sent Damrosch a professionally copied score of his Second Symphony. As he surely might have predicted, it was never returned.

Charles and Harmony Ives
(back row, fourth and fifth
from left) stand with their
family party on their
wedding day in June 1908.

The fact that Ives's abrasive, innovative music had found few champions outside his immediate circle actually proved something of a boon; resigned to the fact that nobody wanted to perform his music, Ives composed with furious energy, not bothering to put his music into final, performable shape. (This proved a hardship, however, to a certain George Price, a professional music copyist whom Ives hired for a time, and who complained constantly and bitterly that he simply could not understand what he was doing. He even went so far as to try to 'correct' some of Ives's harmonic clashes in the attractively rowdy symphonic movement called *The Fourth of July*. But this drew a stern note: 'Mr Price,' Ives implored, 'please don't try to make things nice! All the wrong notes are right'.)

In 1911 Charles and Harmony Ives left New York City and found lodging in the more congenial rural setting of Westchester County immediately to the North. Once again, the change of lifestyle seems to have sparked in Ives a new wave of defiant creativity. It manifested itself immediately in *The Fourth of July* (which was later to be joined with depictions of other American celebrations into 'A Symphony: Holidays'), and into the work considered by many as Ives's masterpiece, the Second, or 'Concord' Sonata, the work a New York critic would later dub 'the greatest music composed by an American'.

Ralph Waldo Emerson, immortalized in the first movement of Ives's 'Concord' Sonata, lived in this spacious home in Concord, Massachusetts.

Autograph page from *The Fourth of July*, part of Ives's collection of tone-poems celebrating the American holidays, showing his fussy, precise instructions to the music copyist

We need not dig too deeply to uncover the bonds of kinship
between Ives and the New England Transcendentalists, who flourished around Concord, Massachusetts in the 1830s, bound together
by belief in the supremacy of instinct over formalism, and in the
eventual emergence of a naturalistic American culture based on
native precepts. Many of America's most distinguished writers were
adherents: Ralph Waldo Emerson, poet and philosopher; Nathaniel
Hawthorne, novelist and fantasist, virtually the inventor of
science fiction; the Alcotts, whose novels captured the comforts of
the budding American middle class. And there was Henry David
Thoreau, abjuring the artifice of urban convention in favour of the
freedom of life at his lakeside; more than in anyone, his spirit found
its avatar in Charles Edward Ives, scornful of the narrowness of the
European musical formality, blending the rough-cut catchpenny
tunes of country brass bands and hymn-singers into his own high
art. 'Thoreau was a great musician', Ives wrote, 'not because he
played the flute but because he didn't have to go to Boston to hear
"the Symphony". The rhythms of his prose, were there nothing
else, would determine his value as a composer.'

Ives had begun an 'Emerson' Overture while still living in New
York; it was an elaborate piece that even went through one metamorphosis as a piano concerto. 'The orchestra was the world and
people hearing', he later wrote, 'and the piano was Emerson'. In a
manner similar to Emerson's way of constructing an essay, its stream
of ideas radiating from a centre, Ives punctuated the piano part
with what he called 'centrifugal cadenzas'. In any case, the overture
was not completed; the cadenzas later turned up as separate
piano studies.

But the spirits of Emerson and his Transcendental colleagues
found their way into the vast sonata, subtitled 'Concord, Mass:
1840–1860', that Ives began in 1911 and tinkered with over the next
four years. The piece obviously meant a great deal to its composer.
We can judge this from his own passionate identification with the
figures in the four movements – Emerson, Hawthorne, the Alcotts
and Thoreau – and also from the intense effort he put into surrounding the work with what amounts to an elaborate statement of faith.
In 1920 he completed *Essays Before a Sonata*, eighty dense and eloquent pages 'written by the composer for those who can't stand his
music – and the music for those who can't stand his essays'. Much of

the text is given over to Ives's fervent denial of the power of music to depict specific personages. The work's fearsome difficulties – it has been called the most technically demanding of all piano works – draw both the pianist and the audience into a tight bonding with the music. The rolling rhetoric of Emerson fills every page of the sonata's first movement; startling passages describing the unruly Hawthorne require the pianist to whomp down, with a block of wood, on several keys at once; and the serene finale even calls for a flute player in an optional few measures, a portrait of Thoreau himself at one of his favourite pastimes. 'Some say "Why choose local authors as a reason for music?"' Ives wrote. 'People will say you are provincial … God lives somewhere in the Heavens, but ain't He universal? Emerson lives in Massachusetts, but he's as universal as any writer.'

Despite Ives's half-hearted protest, the idea of assigning personal characters to his abstract music continued to fascinate him. His First String Quartet, written at Yale, had been a tone-painting of revivalist hymn-meetings – getting out of hand now and then but remaining affectionately close to its source materials. A second quartet, written at about the same time as the 'Concord' Sonata carried the notion a step farther; each of the four characters were creatures of Ives's invention, and his later notes on the work gave him the chance to exercise one of his pet preachments, against those timid souls who found his music hard to take. To Ives these naysayers were invariably 'old ladies', whether male or female (the most hidebound of his invented critics bore the demeaning surname of 'Rollo'). He wrote:

A better Second String Quartet … is one of the best things I have, but the old ladies (male and female) don't like it anywhere at all. It makes them mad … It used to come over me … that music had been and still was an emasculated art. The string quartet music got more weak, trite and effeminate … I started a string quartet score, half mad, half in fun … making those men fiddlers get up and do something like men.

Ives subtitled the work 'S[tring] Q[uartet] for 4 men who converse, argue (in re "politick"), fight, shake hands, shut up – and then walk up the mountain-side to view the firmament'. In his notes on the Second Quartet, written twenty years later, Ives endowed the four players with names; the second violinist, who is made to express the most traditional of the work's tunes is, in fact, named Rollo; his job is to maintain 'traditional' order among the aggressively hetero- geneous parts. Ives allotted Rollo several solos within the work, and endowed them with markings like 'andante emasculata' and 'largo sweetola'. He comes into his own particularly in the second move- ment, which Ives subtitled 'Arguments'. The players do, indeed, argue; each has a distinct and separate melodic line, while Rollo seems always to champion some kind of traditional musical order. Towards the end of the movement Ives, as was his wont, adds a number of musical quotations: American patriotic songs and even a snatch from Tchaikovsky's 'Pathétique' Symphony. The final movement ends in serene, transcendental calm.

If the 'Concord' Sonata and the Second Quartet represent the quintessence of Ives's adventurous musical visions, they are but two landmarks among many in what was to prove the composer's last decade of major compositional effort. The year 1911, when the major work on both scores was taking place, also witnessed the start of the creation of at least two more works of utmost importance and value: the three movements known variously as 'First Orchestral Set', A 'New England' Symphony and, more commonly, *Three Places in New England* – sublime music by any name – and the Fourth Symphony, most complex of all Ives's orchestral works.

The *Three Places* – The St Gaudens Statue in Boston Common, General Putnam's Camp in Redding Connecticut, and The Housatonic at Stockbridge (Massachusetts) – are the triumph of Ives's ventures into pure orchestral colour. The shimmer on the Housatonic ranks beside the sea depictions of Debussy (for whom, however, Ives had little use); more remarkable, however, are the goings-on at Putnam's Camp, with strollers and marchers parading in simulta- neously different rhythms: murderous for the conductor, fascinating for the listener.

The Fourth Symphony took shape over several years until its completion in 1916. More even than the Putnam's Camp movement or the arguments that go on in the Second String Quartet, this symphony achieves an amazing, layered texture. Two or three en- sembles piled on one another, each in a different tonality and rhythm, produce a tangle of musical thoughts. Through the tangle one can pick out a familiar hymn-tune or two; a chorus is on hand to sing some of these. Musical events seem to dash in and out of focus, as in

Charles Ives at thirty-nine, photographed in New York's Battery Park. By 1913 he had virtually abandoned composing, but his music was still unknown.

some dense contrapuntal dream. Not until 1965 did the work achieve a full performance, under the single-handed mastery of Leopold Stokowski; most subsequent performances tend to enlist the services of two or more conductors, to nobody's disgrace.

In 1912 the Iveses purchased a farm in West Redding, Connecticut, with a beautiful view over the hills back toward Danbury of blessed memory. The couple designed the new farmhouse and did most of the building. They had no children of their own, but compensated by lifetimes of charity work in orphanages and similar child-help institutions. Another small house on their property was eventually given over to accommodate needy families, chosen by a local chari-table organization, for rural vacations one month at a time. One of the families had a sickly baby girl who seemed to thrive in the country air; the Iveses persuaded the parents to leave the child behind, and in time she was adopted as Edith Osborne Ives (1914–56).

At Redding Ives brought several musical projects to completion. The insurance business was going well, but Ives still found time for

Charles Ives with his
adopted daughter Edith
Osborne Ives, from a
passport photograph taken
in 1924

his other life as well, at his worktable virtually every evening, usually working on half-a-dozen unfinished scores at once. At Redding, too, Ives completed the most ambitious of his considerable song legacy, a striding, delirious setting of Vachel Lindsay's *General Booth Enters Heaven*, with the Salvation Army's beloved founder met at the Pearly Gates by a glorious contingent of brass-band tunes (all played, of course, by the hard-working piano accompanist). Now and then, but not often, he managed to persuade a few friendly musicians to hear, or even perform, some of his scores. For example, he recorded:

*Dave and Max Smith were … men I respected and got along with,
except when it came to music. I played over the Third Symphony and
Max asked how I had 'got so modern. It's even worse than ten years ago!
How CAN you like horrible sounds like that?' Max at the time had been
for a good many years the music critic on the* New York American.

Shocked by the outbreak of war in Europe, the Iveses decided
that life on their farm was needlessly isolating, most of all from the
heightened demands the insurance business was bound to pose in
wartime; they took another New York apartment for winter months,
returning to Redding from May to November. On 7 May 1915, the
Germans torpedoed the liner *Lusitania* off the Irish coast, with terrible loss of life; the world responded in shock. Late that afternoon, as
Ives waited for an elevated train in a downtown Manhattan station, a
barrel-organ player on the street below stuck up a hymn tune, 'In the
Sweet Bye-and-Bye'. Immediately, as Ives later noted in a memoir, the
crowd upstairs took up the tune – 'as though every man in New York
might be joining in'. 'Then the first train came in', Ives wrote, 'and
everybody crowded in and the song died out'. The memory of this
episode found its place in the Second Orchestral Set, in a movement
titled *From Hanover Square North, at the End of a Tragic Day, the Voice
of the People Again Arose.*

In the autumn of 1915 Ives began to sketch what could have been
the most grandiose of his spacious compositions, a 'Universe'
Symphony, subtitled 'The Earth and the Firmament', scored for two
or more orchestras, '… a striving to contemplate in tones, rather than
in music as such … the mysterious beginnings of all things, from
the great roots of life to the spiritual eternities'. Ives worked on the
'Universe' Symphony sporadically until 1928, but nothing of substance resulted and nearly half of the sketches are now considered
lost. The USA entered the war in April 1917; Ives became an ardent
participant in the Red Cross and Liberty Loan fund drives and even
applied to serve as ambulance driver at the front. In September, at
a Liberty Loan meeting, he argued arduously for the issuance of
small-value bonds so that ordinary people could contribute to the
war effort, and won his case. A year later, however, at the height of
his active participation in the war effort and while struggling to
put his own scattered manuscripts into some kind of order, a severe

Following page, the final
moments of the steamship
Lusitania, torpedoed from a
German submarine on 7 May
1915, as recreated by the
New York newspaper artist
Charles Dixon: reaction to the
event is commemorated in
Ives's Second Orchestral Set.

heart attack put an end for a time to both his business and musical activities; he never truly enjoyed good health for the rest of his life.

At the age of forty-four, Charles Ives was obliged by his weakening constitution, brought on by a succession of heart attacks, to end the career that stamped him as the most innovative, original and indefinable composer of serious music his country had produced. Indeed, he had been the first to prove that the phrase 'American composer' did not constitute a contradiction in terms. He would live another thirty-six years; even without significant compositional activity he would see his prestige in the musical world increase and, at the end, explode into full if tardy glory. Serious composition had taken up only twenty of his fourscore years, but he never really stopped being a composer.

The heart attacks did serve one useful purpose, in making Ives aware of his responsibility to future generations of musicians, and aware of the time when, he firmly believed, his music would finally be discovered, played and understood. He resumed as soon as he could the task of putting his music, most of which existed only as hastily sketched manuscripts, into some kind of order. On a recuperative holiday in the North Carolina mountains, he made fair ink copies of the 'Concord' Sonata, and also completed the remarkable *Essays Before a Sonata*, to serve as a bridge between the sonata itself and the world which would someday discover it. More than an explanatory programme note, the *Essays* embody and define Ives's passionate adherence to the principles of Transcendentalism; in doing so, they also constitute a map of Ives's own soul. In 1920 both the sonata and the essay were published at Ives's expense; he sent free copies to many musicians he hoped to interest, at long last, in his music. A year later he assembled more than 100 songs that he had composed since his early days, and underwrote their publication and distribution as well.

Disillusioned by America's rightward political drift after the war, its rejection of the League of Nations and the repudiation in 1920 of Woodrow Wilson's idealistic visions, Ives expended some of his waning energy in speaking out on his own formulas for saving the world. A song titled *November 2, 1920* (the date of the Presidential election in which the ineffectual conservative Warren Harding was elected) sets Ives's own sardonic text condemning Americans for turning their backs on liberal principles. In a rambling essay from the

same year, called *The Majority*, Ives spoke out, in terms as abrasive
as some of his musical experiments, against the fallacy of democracy.
Let all laws be decided, he proposed, not by legislative bodies but
by popular referendum; only then can a 'freedom' worthy of its
name exist.

Much of Ives's time in the years following his stroke was given over
to reorganization rather than to creation. 'He came downstairs one
day with tears in his eyes', Harmony Ives remembered, 'and said he
couldn't seem to compose any more – nothing went right'. The Iveses
made several trips to Europe, merely as tourists; if America had still
not discovered Ives's music by the mid 1920s, there was even less
chance of his being recognized abroad. In 1930, his health and sight
seriously undermined, Ives retired from his insurance business.

Gradually, however, the pall of obscurity over Ives's musical
presence began to lighten, at least at home. American singers, finally
emboldened to regard their own country's music as a legitimate
pursuit, discovered in the Ives legacy a huge repertory of songs of
tremendous stylistic variety: elegant love lyrics, reworkings of hymn
tunes and lively pseudo-revivalist pieces full of hollering and shouting. At a Los Angeles concert in 1933, the energetic contralto
Radianna Pazmor sang and recorded Ives's *General William Booth
Enters Heaven*. It was one of the first recordings of anything by Ives:
a gateway to his rediscovery.

By then a new generation of younger American composers had
started to discover Ives. One of them, Elliott Carter, remained
a friend and advocate for the rest of Ives's life. Henry Cowell had
begun a magazine called *New Music*, which in 1929 published one
whole movement from Ives's Fourth Symphony. Cowell also
called Ives's music to the attention of the Russian émigré Nicolas
Slonimsky, whose Boston Chamber Orchestra had become a
bastion for new musical ideas.

Born in St Petersburg in 1894, raised in the conservative milieu
of Russian conservatory life under Alexander Glazunov, Slonimsky
became one of the world's most ardent new-music advocates. As
secretary to Serge Koussevitzky during his time as head of the Boston
Symphony, Slonimsky had the interesting task of writing out
simplified versions of new works so that Koussevitzky could read
them and maintain his reputation as a patron of the new. By so

doing, Slonimsky himself absorbed the passion for innovation that his employer professed, and when the two parted company the young Russian began producing his own programmes. Slonimsky gave the world première of *Three Places in New England* in 1931 and *The Fourth of July* in 1932; both works were later performed in Paris, also under Slonimsky's direction. The conductor comments in *Charles Ives Remembered*, the oral history compiled by Vivian Perlis:

> *It was no secret that Ives financed my concerts in Paris, Berlin and Budapest, which included ... his music but also other music. He insisted on adding an extra thousand dollars, and so he gave me a letter of credit for four thousand dollars, which was an amazing sum of money in 1931 ...*

As the music emerged so, of course, did the critics. Slonimsky's Paris performances, at the first all-American concerts that city had ever encountered, were energetically, if not always happily, received: '[he] seems to have forged himself a style which, by its boldness, puts him among the precursors. Beside his compatriots, he seems the most spontaneously gifted ...' So wrote the Parisian critic Paul Le Flem in *Comœdia*. Others were more reserved. 'If it be true that Charles Ives composed "New England Scenes" before acquaintance with Stravinsky's *Le Sacre du printemps*', wrote the *New York Times*'s Paris correspondent Henri Prunières, 'he ought to be recognized as an originator.' In fact, nine-tenths of Ives's score was completed before a note of *Le Sacre* had been heard in Paris, let alone in Connecticut. Boston's Philip Hale condemned Slonimsky's programmes, which seemed to him to represent all American composers as 'wild-eyed anarchists'.

Ives manipulated the transition from obscurity to antipathy none too easily. In 1932, stung by Hale's review, and by the general hostility to new music manifested by the *New York Times*'s critic W. J. Henderson, he began to dictate what he called, simply, 'Memos', a running (some might say 'wildly leaping') conflation of biographical notes (all the way back to George Ives's Danbury band concerts), valuable programme notes on virtually every work of consequence he considered worth preserving, rejoinders to critics benevolent and hostile, and some profound thoughts on how much worse off the world could have been if Charlie Ives had not come along at all.

Opposite, sketch of an elderly but spry Charles Ives by Benedict F. Dolbin

The jabs at critics make wonderful reading and could, of course, be written by other composers, against other mistuned pairs of ears, at any time in musical history from the Middle Ages to the present. Hale ('a nice and dear old lady in Boston – with pants on, often – who sells his nice opinions about music and things') and Henderson (dubbed Rollo, 'who has taken a great deal of money for many years for telling people what he knows and hears – whatever that means') are the chief villains, for reasons at least partly of their own making. Writing in 1931 Hale, for example, found in Ives's *Three Places in New England* (completed in 1914) strong influences of Paul Hindemith (who began composing in 1920).

Dictating the 'Memos' (to a succession of secretaries, each less efficient than the previous) occupied Ives for three months in 1932; the pianist and scholar John Kirkpatrick accomplished the Herculean task of piecing them together for publication in 1972. The Iveses spent another full year as sightseers in Europe; by the time of their return in July 1933 Ives found himself the centre of a small but grow-ing knot of enthusiasts. Aaron Copland had produced a programme of Ives songs, and that had sparked many other performances. Critics, especially those outside the established American daily press, came around. Paul Rosenfeld, probably the most eloquent of all critics attuned to the music of their own time, had deplored Ives's orches-trations when he heard a workshop reading of two movements from the Fourth Symphony, in 1927. By 1932, however, he had heard Slonimsky's performances, and succumbed to *Three Places in New England* as 'the freshest, most eloquent and solid orchestral pieces composed in America'. 'The forces conveyed by his music', Rosenfeld wrote, 'are deeply, typically American. They are the essences of a practical people, abrupt and nervous and ecstatic in their movements … manifested sometimes in a bucolic irony and burlesque and sometimes in a religious and mystical elevation, but almost invariably in patterns that have a paroxysmal suddenness and abruptness and violence …'

Not always with Rosenfeld's eloquence, but with his conviction, the awareness of Ives's stature spread, in successive paroxysmal outbursts of superlatives. Another milestone occurred on 20 January 1939, when John Kirkpatrick gave the first complete performance of the 'Concord' Sonata in New York's Town Hall. The audience was small, but the cry raised by Lawrence Gilman's review in the *New*

JOHN
KIRKPATRICK
Piano Recital

TOWN HALL
113 West 43rd Street

FRIDAY EVENING AT 8:30

JANUARY 20th

In January, 1939, a quarter-century after its completion, Ives's 'Concord' Sonata had its first complete performance, at New York's Town Hall by John Kirkpatrick, as advertised on this poster.

Sonata in C major, Op. 53   BEETHOVEN

  I. allegro con brio
  II. Introduzione, adagio molto
      Rondo, allegretto moderato—prestissimo

Concord, Mass., 1840-60   CHARLES E. IVES

SECOND PIANOFORTE SONATA (1911-15)
("an attempt to present one person's impression of the spirit of transcendentalism that is associated in the minds of many with Concord, Mass., of over a half century ago")

I. Emerson ("a composite picture or impression")

II. Hawthorne (an "extended fragment" reflecting "some of his wilder, fantastical adventures into the half-childlike, half-fairylike phantasmal realms")

III. The Alcotts ("a sketch")

IV. Thoreau ("an autumn day of Indian summer at Walden")

FIRST PERFORMANCE

STEINWAY PIANO

Tickets: Box seats $2.75, Orchestra $2.20, $1.65, $1.10, Balcony $.83
Tax included   At Box Office

Management RICHARD COPLEY, Steinway Bldg., 113 West 57th St., New York, N. Y.

York Herald-Tribune ('the greatest music composed by an American ...') necessitated a second performance, on 24 February, this time to a packed house.

Charles Ives's musical legacy began to fall into place. Chamber groups hunted down the four violin sonatas, works from around 1910 peppered with quotations from American fiddle tunes and hymns.

Singers fell hungrily upon the songs in their infinite variety; Radianna
Pazmor hurling out the 'zing-bam-boom' refrains in *General Booth*
even became something of a party record. (One record exists, by the
way, of Ives himself, caterwauling his wartime anthem 'They Are
There!' It has been worked into a piece of the same name by the
Kronos Quartet.) In Los Angeles, the dynamic new-music enthusiast
Peter Yates started a new-music series on the roof of his Hollywood
home, and pushed a considerable amount of Ives's music into the
awareness of his audiences; Ives sent along free copies of his music,
and some money as well.

There was a certain monotony in Ives's gradual accession of
world stages. Headlines in the 1930s seemed like a persistent
drumbeat: 'Charles Ives Emerges'; 'Tardy Recognition'; 'Charles Ives
is Rediscovered'; 'Belated Tom-Tom for Genius', etc. The beat
intensified by the late 1940s. Ives finally consented to allow his
friends, Henry and Sidney Cowell, to compile a biography; the final
product, far too short perhaps but filled with fondness and care for
the subject matter, did not appear until 1955. (Between 1936 and
1940, when Henry Cowell was imprisoned in California on a morals
charge brought by a young man, Ives turned his back on his old
friend and refused to contribute to a legal fund or write a letter on
Cowell's behalf. After Cowell's release and marriage, however, the
friendship resumed as if nothing had happened.)

On 5 April 1946 the composer Lou Harrison, who in his early
years had been a student of Cowell's in San Francisco, conducted the
New York Little Symphony in the first performance of Ives's Third
Symphony, the first major première of a work by Ives since the
Slonimsky performances of 1932. This time the press was present in
force; the *New York Times*'s Olin Downes wrote of the work's 'virility,
originality and essential modernity'. Considering that the work was
by then forty-three years old and only belatedly honoured by the
Pulitzer judges, Ives had earned the right to his irascible rejoinder
about 'prizes [being] the badges of mediocrity'. Harrison and Cowell
had prepared the score themselves from Ives's muddled manuscript;
the composer was by then ailing and nearly blind. The Second String
Quartet also received its first performance in 1946. One by one, the
scattered shards of Charles Ives's creative legacy assumed their rightful
place in public recognition.

Charles and Harmony Ives at
their home in West Redding,
Connecticut in 1948

It all happened too late to afford Ives himself much pleasure.
Embittered by the years of unjustified neglect and the hostility of the
most powerful of the nation's critics, Ives burrowed ever deeper into
the cocoon of self-willed isolation. Musicians and composers who
had once been close friends, and apostles to the outside world, found
themselves the targets of wrathful outbursts followed by clumsy
overtures of reconciliation: this happened not only to Cowell but also
to Elliott Carter. Only one composer seemed to enjoy access to the
small and gloomy inner circle: Carl Ruggles, another self-willed loner
whose music embodied much of Ives's saltiest dissonances. Charlotte
Ruggles recalled, and Harmony Ives corroborated, the night when
the two old boys suddenly dropped all pretence of elderly dignity and
marched around the Ives's dining-room table shouting out an old
American march tune that Ives had once appropriated in one of his
early works. The 93-year-old Ruggles reminisced during an interview
in 1969:

The Sun Treader, Thomas
Hart Benton's 1934 portrait
of Ives's great friend, the
composer Carl Ruggles,
was named after Ruggles's
best-known work.

I heard him play at West Redding. 'I never heard a better pianist in my life. I was there when Ives threw the 'Browning' Overture clear across the dining-room floor. He was so sick then. 'To hell with the goddamn thing', he said. He'd swear something terrible. He could even beat me swearing. He said 'the goddamn thing is no good'. I got up, went over to get that score back. I said 'I don't think I would say that, when I hear such phrases as here and here and here. Such magnificent music as that'. He said 'you think that?'

On the heels of the Third Symphony's great success, the rest of Ives's orchestral works tumbled off the shelf, one by one. Leonard Bernstein conducted the Second Symphony with the New York Philharmonic in 1951; the enterprising Richard Bales removed the wraps from the First Symphony at a concert in Washington, DC in April 1953. Antal Dorati and the Minneapolis Symphony introduced the 'Holidays' Symphony (compiled from the orchestral movements *Thanksgiving and/or Forefathers Day, Washington's Birthday, Decoration Day* and *The Fourth of July*) in April 1954. However, it would take the Fourth Symphony, the most complex of all of Ives's works, another eleven years to gain its first hearing, in the legendary 1965 performance conducted by Leopold Stokowski.

Leonard Bernstein, photographed here in the early 1960s, was largely responsible for the emergence of Ives's orchestral music from undeserved obscurity.

Characteristically, Ives himself attended none of these events. Even though he could occasionally be persuaded to take in a symphonic concert or piano recital, to the end of his life he studiously shunned the experience of hearing his own music. He never owned a radio or phonograph, although he did allow himself the unaccustomed indulgence of tuning in on Bernstein's broadcast of the Second Symphony, on a small radio in the kitchen. He grew weaker year by year, but let it be known – however reluctantly – that the belated discovery of his music was a source of joy and pride.

On 19 May 1954, Ives was recovering from a minor operation when he suddenly suffered a stroke. His daughter Edith later wrote that she and her mother sat at her father's bedside, holding hands, as the spirit serenely ebbed from his body.

The poet Louis Untermeyer came to know Ives in the 1940s; Ives had set some of his poetry to music. Untermeyer's memory of their time together can stand as the ultimate portrait.

His presence impressed me. There are a few people who have presence per se, not because they're handsome or because they're powerful-looking, but because they have a quiet dignity, a kind of self-assurance. He knew

Leopold Stokowski conducted many first performances of difficult contemporary works including, in 1965, the premiere of Ives's Fourth Symphony.

*what he had done. He knew what he was, and that was that. He took it
for granted, and I took it for granted. He didn't have to boast. He didn't
have to talk about his published work. I spoke a little about it, and he
sort of waved it away. I have had that with a few people only. Robert
Frost was one. He had that quality, too. I felt it immediately with Ives.*

The question of the intrinsic quality of Ives's music remains unanswered. His importance as a musical pioneer is, of course, beyond
challenge; he can be reckoned the inventor of a national American
music, built out of the indigenous music of his own country and
manipulated in an individualistic manner; we can say the same of
Mussorgsky in Russia or Smetana and Janáček in Czechoslovakia.
The daring of his manipulations, furthermore, advanced the frontiers
of the musical language. The sheer arrogance of his musical technique
is both thrilling and appalling: the bravado with which he could
smash great blocks of musical substance against one another, creating
a simultaneity that erased all sense of the traditional boundaries of the
musical language. The argumentations among the four participants
in the Second String Quartet, the clashing rhythms in the *Putnam's
Camp* movement of the *Three Places in New England*, the wild con-
frontations throughout the Fourth Symphony (which demand two
conductors for proper realization, or one conductor with two heads):
these constitute a major step into the unknown. Almost every serious
composer currently active in the USA – whether 'serious', jazz-
oriented or rock star – will claim descent from Ives to any probing
interviewer. Only a single composer in Ives's own time bears any kind
of resemblance to his musical ideals: his fellow Yankee, Carl Ruggles,
who developed an Ivesian method for creating abrasive contrapuntal
textures, and who shared Ives's delight in creating musical tributes
to the Transcendental poets and philosophers of an earlier time.

Ives stands at both the beginning and end of a musical line. He
abjured traditional German values and condemned Haydn, Mozart
and Brahms as music for 'old ladies, like Toscanini'. Yet his mind
turned to traditional German forms, symphony, string quartet and
sonata, as the logical vessels for musical thought. Even the single-
movement works, the jocular show-off pieces like *The Gong on the
Hook and Ladder* and the tone poems like the New England Sketches
and *Central Park in the Dark*, echo the tendencies of the German

romantics. Most of the songs seem like the furtherance of the German Lied tradition, except for the few based on Ives's own political tracts and the one, *General Booth*, which is more like a tone poem that accidentally became a song. The pioneers who came after him tended to shy away from quartets and symphonies; they brewed their own vintages, and made their own containers as well.

Some clear-eyed cynicism is needed. Sources close to Ives – Elliott Carter for one – saw him alter sketches, adding dissonant touches to enhance his image as an innovator before his time; we have to wonder how far back Ives's 'modernity' really goes. Should this matter, however, given the strength of the final product? Is it important that not all the contrapuntal amazement of the Fourth Symphony was composed at the same time, or can the music itself stand alone? Instinctive, spontaneous or contrived, the devices in his music place Ives in the midst of the twentieth-century pioneering spirit. Run down the list of the devices that twentieth-century composers have devised to torture the timid souls in their audiences; you will find them also in Ives's music, installed there by accident or design.

Polytonality? Almost any page in the Fourth Symphony presents a profusion of different tonalities evolving along separate paths, like a newly opened tin of worms. Atonality? Even that disputed opening of the First Symphony, which understandably sent Horatio Parker into a rage, abandons any traditional sense of 'keyishness' in favour of youthful anarchy. Microtonality? A whole sonata, quite a delightful piece in fact, is composed for two pianos tuned a quarter-tone apart.

Slowly, Ives's music makes its way onto the international stage. A Moscow orchestra has recorded *The Unanswered Question*, the one work of Ives known to almost every Russian musician. Orchestras in Amsterdam, Oslo and Tokyo have recorded the music. The quiet, small Third Symphony is in the repertory of the Academy of St Martin-in-the-Fields, alongside Vivaldi and Handel. The 'rediscovered' Second Symphony, on which Bernstein rode to glory as the heroic rescuer of a neglected avant-garde pioneer (and recorded three or four times), is a matter somewhat more troublesome, since it is really something of a backward work, suitable to Bernstein's conservative image more than to the hell-raising Ives.

The masterpieces among Ives's works – the brief, haunting *Unanswered Question*, the intense, mysterious Fourth Symphony and

Opposite, Charles Ives, photographed in 1950 on a visit to Danbury, his native city. Already greatly weakened in body if not in mind, he was to live on for a further four years.

the grandiose 'Concord' Sonata – have no ancestry; they are the embodiment of a deep and dedicated creative spirit, original and visionary. Audiences are still, only now, discovering the rolling, intense rhetoric of the Emerson movement in 'Concord', or the deep, spiritual calm in the gorgeously-named *The Housatonic at Stockbridge*, last of the New England pieces. The music abides.

Max Weber: *Rush Hour,
New York*, 1915

The production of a piece such as Ionisation
*was indubitably in the evolutionary order of
things, predestined both by the direction of
Varèse's own development and by the
development of musical feeling and musical
resources during the last century and a half.*

Paul Rosenfeld,
Discoveries of a Music Critic, 1928

Edgard Varèse

The pioneer's responsibility is to lay down pathways where none previously existed. For a composer born and educated in America, the role of pioneer was easily assumed. For Charles Ives, for example, it was simply a matter of blotting out the minuscule amount of European training that had washed over him early in his career, and then finding his own way towards a native American musical language. For the composer born and trained abroad in one of Europe's music centres, however, assuming the role of pioneer involved a drastic process of rejection: turning one's back on a traditional European education in order to put down new roots in America. In the case of Edgard Varèse, it helped that a warehouse fire destroyed virtually everything he had created up to the time of his emigration to America, but it is likely that Varèse might have lit the blaze himself had not others done the job. Presented by the God of Fire with an open roadway towards a second start in America after a series of European discouragements, he went on to produce music so innovative as to suggest a drastic realignment in the very definition of the aesthetic experience. Even the term 'music' seemed, to Varèse, a hobbling concept; instead, he considered his creation 'organized sound'.

Henri Varèse, an engineer by profession, had no intention of allowing his son a musical career. The family moved from Paris to Turin soon after Edgard was born (22 December 1883); the boy was raised by maternal relatives in Burgundy. He loved that part of the world, and travelled happily back and forth from Le Villars, a village near Tournus, to Paris to visit his grandfather, who ran a bistro in the capital city. His first major composition, *Bourgogne*, was a tone poem in honour of the region of his happy childhood.

At the age of nine, the boy was returned to his parents. Any budding desires toward a musical career were stifled by his father who, as Edgard later remembered, had gone so far as to throw a shroud over the family piano and to keep the key hidden. He loathed

The young Edgard Varèse (rear) in Turin, with his two younger brothers Maurice and Renaldo, and Corinne, the younger of his two sisters

his father, and the feeling seems to have been mutual. The elder Varèse was given to inflicting corporal punishment at little provocation. Much later, Edgard's widow Louise, in a biography of her husband, reports to have heard him mutter, over and over as a sort of refrain in both English and French, 'I should have killed that *salaud*'. All that Henri's hostility seemed to accomplish was to make his young son rebellious; surreptitiously, Edgard attended music classes at the Turin Conservatory and even sat in for a time in the percussion section of the school's orchestra. Eventually, the elder Varèse came to realize his powerlessness to control his son, and allowed his music lessons in composition, piano and percussion to continue. Edgard's mother died when he was fourteen; on her deathbed, she warned her son that Henri Varèse was 'an assassin'. He remained with his father – 'a kind of Prussian drill-master', was one of his kinder descriptions –

The ancient abbey of
St Philibert in Tournus, the
town in Burgundy where the
young Edgard Varèse
lived with relatives for
several years, and which
inspired *Bourgogne*, his first
large-scale orchestral score

for four more years, in a state of mounting belligerence. At nineteen, seeing his father raise a hand to his stepmother, Edgard administered a thrashing to the older man and left home for good.

Paris in 1903 seethed with musical excitement. Debussy's *Pelléas et Mélisande*, with its haunting musical reflection of half-statements and shadows, had attained the status of *scandale*. The battle lines were drawn. The conservative attitude towards music, seeking to maintain the tradition of the symphony (which in any case the French had not really mastered since the time of Hector Berlioz), was typified by the greying master Vincent D'Indy, whose music seemed an uneasy mix of Wagnerian harmony and academic rigidity. Opposed to this were the adherents of Debussy's free-form colouristic experiments and his passion for seeking new inspiration in music of exotic lands. Varèse attended classes at the two most prestigious Parisian music schools, the Schola Cantorum and the Conservatoire, but found the level of pedagogy at both institutions stifling and old-fashioned, more concerned with systems of composition than free expression. In Paris, however, he gained entry into the avant-garde circles frequented by both musicians and visual artists. He became a devout follower of Debussy, and a friend as well.

The French composer and teacher Vincent D'Indy, who represented the conservative side of Parisian musical life around 1900

The actress Suzanne Bing, briefly married to Varèse during his student days in Paris, and their young daughter Claude; Claude is also seen, *below*, with her proud father, a starving Parisian artist.

Italian-born and adoptive Berliner Ferruccio Busoni, whose radical writings on the aesthetics of music, as well as his own compositions, inspired the young Varèse

The year 1907 saw two major events in the life of the 22-year-old
Varèse. One was his marriage to the actress Suzanne Bing; the couple
bedded down in an unheated Paris flat and produced a daughter. The
other was Varèse's discovery of a tract, *A New Aesthetic of Music*, by
the visionary Ferruccio Busoni, composer, performer and teacher (and
a virtuoso in all three fields). Busoni, Italian born but German by
adoption, sounded the call for a drastic revision of the basic concepts
of harmony and melody that had guided composers since the Middle
Ages. He advanced the possibilities of scales built from other than
the familiar half-and whole-step intervals, and also of new instruments capable of creating sounds of which previous composers had
only dreamed. 'Music was born free', Busoni proclaimed, 'and to
win freedom is its destiny'.

Varèse was enthralled by this call to freedom, amazed and excited
'to find there was someone beside myself, and a musician at that,
who believed this. It gave me courage to go on …' He packed up his
small family and moved to Berlin, where Busoni's classes were luring
progressive-minded students from all over the world. Busoni accepted
the young Frenchman as a kindred spirit; Varèse also earned the
respectful attention of none other than Richard Strauss, who pulled
strings to get a performance of *Bourgogne* at Berlin's Blüthner
Hall on 15 December 1910. The critics received the work as 'infernal
noise, cat-music', and thus the career of Edgard Varèse was
auspiciously launched.

By early 1913 the marriage had failed. Varèse and Suzanne separated amicably, she to return to her acting career in Paris, he to
remain in Berlin a few months more, the daughter to live with her
maternal grandmother. By then Varèse had created a large body of
music, most of it orchestral tone poems and one opera, *Oedipus and
the Sphinx*, little of it noticed by the musical world. He stored most
of his manuscripts in a Berlin warehouse; as luck would have it,
the warehouse was torched during the Socialist uprisings in Berlin
in 1919, apparently to Varèse's great relief. He kept the score of
Bourgogne for a few more years, but eventually put that, too, to
the torch.

In May 1913 Varèse returned to Paris in time to attend the
famous première of Stravinsky's *Rite of Spring* and to experience its
concomitant *scandale*. In Paris he was welcomed back into avant-

garde circles, worked on projects with the surrealist painter and poet Jean Cocteau, and looked in on the inventor René Bertrand, who was exploring early ideas for an electric tone-producing instrument, which, under the name of 'Dynaphone', would not be completed until 1927. At the outbreak of war, Varèse joined the French army, but was quickly discharged because of a lifelong breathing difficulty. In 1915 he sailed for New York, convinced that the artistic freedom that Busoni had demanded for the arts might be more profitably sought on the other side of the Atlantic.

Varèse arrived in New York with ninety dollars in his pocket and a sheaf of letters of introduction from Europe's artistic élite. In his last few months in Europe he had begun to make a name as a conductor. He had enjoyed considerable success with a concert in Prague devoted entirely to contemporary music, and his plan for New York was to continue in that vein, to establish himself as a conductor with a particular leaning towards new works hitherto unheard by American audiences. He applied for American citizenship in 1916, and was eventually successful. His American conducting début in 1917, while not exactly contemporary in outlook, had its sensational aspects: a performance of Hector Berlioz's Requiem on something like the grand scale its composer had stipulated: a chorus of 300 and an orchestra of 150, deployed in the vast space of New York's Hippodrome Theatre. The concert was well received; the critic Paul Rosenfeld, who had also been one of the first critics to discover and write perceptibly about the music of Charles Ives, detected in Varèse 'the inspiration of genius'.

The promise inherent in that New York début did not, however, materialize as planned. In 1919 Varèse became conductor of the New Symphony Orchestra, a co-operative in which the players shared the profits, if any. Varèse saw the orchestra as the vehicle to bring the essence of European creativity to America, while encouraging native composers as well. In a press conference, he told of glowing plans to honour neglected American composers, but his first programme included no American music at all. The four recent European works – by Debussy, Bartók, Casella and Dupont – earned a hostile reception from both the public and the musicians, both groups resentful at having to learn new scores. One New York critic, confronted with the music of Hungary's Béla Bartók for the first

Following page, the New York skyline as Varèse would have seen it upon his arrival in 1915

time, compared him to Attila the Hun 'in his ability to inspire terror'. Varèse refused to change his orchestral policy, however, and was relieved of his post. 'Too many musical organizations', he wrote, '... are mausoleums, mortuaries for musical reminiscence. They cling to the old and shrink from the new.'

New York – 'banal city and dirty' – also had its rewards. Varèse's first friends included the painter Marcel Duchamp, who had found the notoriety stirred up by his *Nude Descending a Staircase* at New York's 1913 Armory Show so delicious that he decided to stay. The German conductor Karl Muck, adored on the podium of the illustrious Boston Symphony Orchestra (until forced to resign for his failure to preface concerts with the national anthem after America's entry into World War I), became a staunch friend, and introduced Varèse to others in the German-speaking colony, including the violinist Fritz Kreisler. Duchamp also introduced Varèse to several of New York's most generous arts patrons, contacts that were to prove eventually, if not immediately, advantageous. Varèse even enjoyed a brief fling in the burgeoning motion-picture industry, cast in a John Barrymore costume drama as a cuckolded Italian nobleman who poisons his wife's lover.

Varèse, the fiery-eyed intense innovator, as New York saw him in the early 1920s

Best of all, the recently-divorced Varèse fell into the company of a young American writer, Louise Norton; the efficient Marcel Duchamp brought them together in the winter of 1917. It was hardly love at first sight, reported Louise in her memoirs. 'My antipathy gave way to liking and gradually to lifelong devotion. As for Varèse, a casual attraction turned into a need'. Edgard and Louise set up home together; not until 1921, however, when her divorce from a previous marriage became final, were they married.

The initial failure of his conducting ambitions seemed only to increase Varèse's eagerness to serve the cause of new music, his own and the works of other major innovative spirits in America and abroad. His closest friends in New York, aside from the patrons he had charmed into supporting his activities during the lean years, came from the cluster of experimenters in all artistic realms. Duchamp had led him into his own Dadaist group, which also included another self exile, the painter and provocateur Francis Picabia, another veteran of the Armory Show. Varèse was made uneasy by the anarchy of Dada, but he contributed articles to Picabia's magazine *391*.

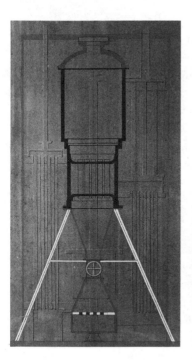

Machine Without Name,
a 1915 gouache, *left,* by
Francis Picabia, another of
the French self-exiles shaking
up the New York art scene;
below, his fellow expatriate
Marcel Duchamp's *Nude
Descending a Staircase
No. 2,* the great *scandale*
of New York's 1913
Armory Show

In 1921 Varèse and the harpist Carlos Salzedo founded the
International Composers' Guild, and this organization was to provide
him, and New York audiences, with their most expansive meeting
ground to date for sampling the music of their own time. The Guild
boasted an impressive letterhead, listing a Board that included
Edgard and Louise Varèse, Salzedo, several prospective patrons and
the Varèse family dentist Maurice Jagendorf, who contributed office
space. The plan was to offer nothing but first performances; not until
its final concert, in April 1927, did it depart from that rubric (and
then only because a majority of its subscribers had petitioned for a
reprise of Varèse's own *Intégrales*.) The Guild came to life swaddled
in a brave declaration of intent:

> ... *Dying is the privilege of the weary. The present-day composers refuse
> to die. They have realized the necessity of banding together and fighting
> for the right of each individual to secure fair and free presentation of his
> work ... The aim of the International Composers' Guild is to centralize
> the works of the day, to group them in programmes intelligently and
> organically constructed. The International Composers' Guild disapproves
> of all 'isms'; denies the existence of schools; recognizes only the individual.*

The formula worked; by the end of the Guild's first season, 1922–3,
the audience had outgrown its small Greenwich Village theatre and
had been forced a move to larger accommodations uptown. For
all the antipathy of the daily newspaper critics, there were others who
recognized the value of these concerts. Chief among them was the
visionary Paul Rosenfeld; he praised the Guild for its 'responsiveness
to the hour, a spirit of initiative, promptitude and willingness combined with an artistic standard of performance'.

Even before the Guild's inaugural concerts, Varèse already had
grander musical projects in mind. Early in 1922 he had begun work
on the score he wanted known as his virginal American flight: a tone
poem to be called *Amériques*, lasting nearly half an hour and enlisting
the services of an America-sized orchestra that called for five of every
woodwind instrument, two tubas and a ten-member percussion
section that included a whip and a siren. Leopold Stokowski and his
Philadelphia Orchestra were set for the première performance; as it
happened, however, financial difficulties in Philadelphia delayed the
arrival of *Amériques* for four years.

Amériques was, for its composer and for the cause of music, a huge step into the unknown; its power to astonish has not yet dimmed. The title, Varèse later wrote, was 'purely sentimental'. The unifying materials are rhythmic rather than melodic: small angular nuggets – like crystals, several writers have suggested – that vibrate and collide within a vast musical continuum. There is no evidence of melodic shapes as traditionally perceived, nor of the consequential progression from one perceptible musical idea to the next. The harmony, too, has little to do with traditional concepts; the tonal progressions in such a work as Stravinsky's *Rite of Spring* seem clear and fathomable beside the jagged outlines in Varèse's vast score.

Was *Amériques* conceived as a tone portrait of Varèse's new-found land or something deeper and more subtle? Varèse wrote:

When I wrote Amériques *I was still under the spell of my first impressions of New York – not only New York seen but, more especially, heard … As a boy, the mere word 'America' meant the unknown. And in this symbolic sense – new world on this planet, in outer space and in the minds of man – I gave this title to the first work I wrote in America. For the first time with my physical ears I heard a sound that had kept recurring in my ears as a boy: a high whistling C sharp. It came to me as I worked in my West-side apartment where I could hear all the river sounds – the lonely foghorns, the shrill peremptory whistles – the whole wonderful river symphony that moved me more than anything had before.*

The plural title, Varèse explained, indicated that *Amériques* was meant to celebrate not merely its composer's discovery of America but 'all discovery, everywhere'.

Amériques eventually had its première, in 1926, under Leopold Stokowski (who along with Boston's Serge Koussevitzky was one of the few symphonic conductors of the time willing to advance the cause of new music). By then the activities of the Guild, and the controversies it stirred – with the press over its choice of composers and within the musical community for its competitiveness with other composer organizations in New York and abroad – had already made Varèse notorious. The eloquent Paul Rosenfeld had fuelled and illuminated the cause; writing after a Guild concert in 1924, he identified Varèse as 'the man destined to lead the art of music onward from Stravinsky into fresh virgin realms of sound'. The new première sent the critics to delve once again into their bestiaries; '*Amériques* seemed to depict the progress of a terrible fire in one of our larger zoos', reported the *New York World*.

Varèse and the Guild had become a regular cause of irritation to the musical scene. Assured for the first time in his life of a convenient outlet for his own music, especially works for small and manageable groups of instrumentalists willing to baptize their own techniques in the dark waters of contemporary innovation, Varèse applied himself more seriously than ever to the career of composer. For the Guild's excellent performing forces his first work was *Offrandes*, a pair of songs for soprano and small orchestra to elegant surrealist texts by Vicente Huidobro and José Juan Tablada, redolent with tropical imagery. *Offrandes* was included on the third and final concert of the Guild's first season, 23 April 1922. Nina Koshetz, a much loved young Russian soprano with a flair for new and challenging music, was the singer. Not since 1910, with the Berlin performance of *Bourgogne*, had Varèse heard a note of his music played in public. This time, furthermore, the audience response was enthusiastic; the first of the two songs had to be repeated. The journal *Musical America* had special praise for the 'fascinating rhythmic colour [achieved] in a little battalion of percussion in which the composer managed the big cymbal'.

The Guild lasted for six years, offering frequent chamber concerts that included works by the European firebrands Stravinsky, Schoenberg and Webern, and music as well from the growing ranks of American originals: Carl Ruggles, Henry Cowell and Varèse himself – but not Charles Ives, already by 1921 cloaked in his mantle of self-willed invisibility. The lesser critics, as usual, rose to all occasions. As the prestige of the Guild increased, and with it the fame of Varèse himself, the press seemed to find ever-increasing delight in the sport of inventing new ways to torment the standard-bearers of the new arts. A performance of Varèse's *Hyperprism* in December 1924 split the critical fraternity only to the extent of an inability to decide whether the roar of the lion (*New York Evening Post*), the braying of goats (*New York Sun*) or the entire menagerie augmented by a boiler factory (*New York Times*) better described the occasion.

At forty-one, Varèse now moved as a hero through New York's small but active progressive arts colony, 'an advanced (or advancing) composer whom nothing could stop', wrote the perceptive Virgil Thomson, who had already made his own mark in musical circles, as a composer with conservative leanings but also as a critic nicely attuned to progressive manifestations. Varèse's American career had proceeded in logical steps: first as a symphonic conductor unflinching even in the face of the mighty Berlioz Requiem; then as a conductor of the most challenging music of his own time, unflinching in the face of public and critical censure; finally as a composer of total originality, an eloquent rebel against the vast tradition out of which he had emerged. Yet he was dissatisfied with the resources at hand, as the poet might curse the limitations of his language or the painter the drabness of the rainbow.

Busoni's tract on the 'new aesthetic', which had lured Varèse to Berlin in 1910, preached the doctrine of an 'eternal harmony', no longer tied to the half-and whole-tone intervals of the familiar major and minor scales that had been the basis of Western harmony for a millennium, but free to employ the infinity of microtones that 'lie in the cracks' between those tones. (Charles Ives, who had frequently expressed his detestation of Varèse and his music for reasons he never made clear – the size of Varèse's ego? his excess of intellectuality? both explanations have been proffered – had also experimented with the 'cracks'. His three pieces for two pianos tuned a quarter-tone apart had been played in New York in 1924. They did nothing, however, to heal the breach between the two men.) With Busoni, the 'eternal harmony' remained a concept on paper; but Claude Debussy had already begun to approach something similar, and in actual practice. As long ago as 1889, when all of Paris thrilled to its first hearing of musicians from the Asian continent and Indonesia, brought to perform at the great Universal Exposition, Debussy had been inspired to push the boundaries of harmony beyond common practice. Debussy's harmonies, his use of a scale built entirely out of whole tones – and, thus, free of the traditional push toward a distinct, identifiable key – had already gone some distance towards translating the libertarian spirit into practice. The teenage Varèse had become enchanted by the implications of Debussy's first steps towards harmonic freedom; he dreamed of moving further along the path.

Later in Paris he had seen René Bertrand's early experiments on an instrument that would eventually emerge as the Dynaphone, capable of producing a continuously variable musical tone controlled by a single operator – the remote ancestor, in other words, of today's wealth of electronic sound-producers. Bertrand's experiments kindled Varèse's imagination; repeatedly, in writings and lectures, he called for a musical future peopled by composer–scientists to expand the inadequate harmonic vocabulary of the time – never mind how well it had served Bach and Mozart – and to move music towards ever more distant horizons. The microtonal future would resound to keyboard instruments that could play not only the half-and whole-tones of traditional practice, but third-and sixth-tones as well, and electric instruments that could destroy all the barriers that fill the insurmountable crack from *do* to *re* and *re* to *mi*.

But that was Varèse's dream of the future. Even within the present inadequacies that clipped his wings, he struggled in search of new ways to expand the tonal possibilities of his music, and met with a certain degree of success. Between 1922 and 1925 he produced three works for the Guild concerts, brief but bristling with original ideas, each a fascinating study in the unconventional use of conventional instruments. None of them more than ten minutes long, they form a vivid picture of a fierce creative spirit banging against the restricting walls of musical tradition.

Hyperprism, four minutes in length but packed with an extraordinary density of invention, was first heard at a Guild concert in March 1923; the usual audience uproar prompted an encore performance on the spot. As with *Amériques* of a year earlier, *Hyperprism* added a siren to the basic instrumental ensemble – not for any narrative or descriptive sense but simply because that instrument provided Varèse with the closest approach to his ideal of a continuously variable musical tone.

Octandre, six minutes long, had its first performance, under Guild auspices, in January 1924. Although scored for eight players (four wind players, three brass and a string bass), the title actually refers to an 'octandrious' (i.e., eight-stamened) flower, which seems to unfold, quietly and enchantingly, through the work's three brief movements. More serene than any known work of Varèse up to that time, its simplicity is deceptive; its unusual instrumental usage (piccolo, oboe and bassoon often playing at the unexpected extremes of their

Opposite, the press and public reaction to Varèse's Hyperprism *at its 1923 première was recorded in this mock-up in the arts magazine* Manuscripts.

[SPECIAL SUPPLEMENT TO MANUSCRIPTS NUMBER 5]

They played a quartet by *Bela Bartok;* someone sang; Marie Miller and Charles Salzedo presented Mr. Salzedo's sonata for harp and piano; someone sang; and Leo Ornstein played beautifully his own sonata and something of Haydn as an encore; and then

EDGAR VARESE

Conducted
His
"HYPERPRISM"
    (*First Performance*)
For
Flute
Clarinet
2 Trumpets
3 French Horns
2 Trombones

It All
Happened
At
The
Klaw
Theatre
Sunday
Night
March
4, 1923

AND PERCUSSION

Played by the Faculty and Pupils of the Dalcroze School of Eurythmics

at the International Composer's Guild

Just as we are going to press so we thought we'd

MENTION IT

He played it once: W I L D   E N T H U S I A S M

A gentleman jumped up on the stage and said:

This is A Serious Work   Those Who Don't Like It

PLEASE GO

A gentleman in the front row orchestra gave him some B A C K   T A L K

Some gentlemen in the G A L L E R Y   SAID:

GET OUT GET OUT

MR. VARESE Began to repeat "Hyperprism" B U T SOMEONE L A U G H E D
MR. VARESE TURNED AROUND AND GLARED while the orchestra stopped and waited
SILENCE HAVING BEEN RESTORED   MR. VARESE PERFORMED

"HYPERPRISM" A SECOND TIME

registers) and constantly shifting rhythms are the work of a
restless explorer.

The following year there was *Intégrales*, wilder and more visionary
within its ten-minute span than any previous compositions of Varèse.
The very concept of the work was cloaked in unreality. 'I planned it for
certain acoustical media not yet available', explained Varèse, 'but which
I knew could be built and would be available'. Scored for winds, brass
and no fewer than seventeen percussion players, the work was greeted at
its Aeolian Hall première (conducted by Leopold Stokowski, on 1
March 1925) by the usual zoological barrage from the press; 'a
combination of early morning in the freight yards, feeding time at the
zoo and a Sixth Avenue trolley rounding a curve, with an intoxicated
woodpecker thrown in for good measure', ranted Britain's implacable
Ernest Newman, serving a year as guest critic on the *New York Evening
Post*. One other of the daily critics, however, seemed this once to cross
over to the enemy camp. Winthrop Tyron of the *Christian Science
Monitor* perceived *Intégrales* as 'the first original score for grand
orchestra that had been made in America since the twentieth century
began. Here we are completely out of the field of borrowed, derived or
imitated musical thought.' By these lights, of course, it had taken a
quarter of a century, and the fashioning hands of an expatriate
Frenchman, to rescue American music from its eclectic past and set it
onto its own individual path. (Very likely Winthrop Tyron, like the rest
of the musical world, had not by 1925 heard a note of Charles Ives.)

One by one, other distinguished musical figures came to recognize
the innovative strength in Varèse, his musical theories and his music.
One notable apostle was Leopold Stokowski, conductor of the
Philadelphia Orchestra since 1912. Stokowski had been a vital force in
the support of new music; he had led the first American performances
of Stravinsky's *Rite of Spring* (in 1922, nine years after the work's Paris
première). The ideals of the Guild appealed to him strongly, and he
made himself available to conduct several of the programmes,
including the première of *Intégrales*. With the splendid forces of his
own orchestra, Stokowski had given the first performance of
Amériques on 9 April 1926 and, a year later, of *Arcana*, Varèse's last
score for full orchestra.

Arcana bore on its title page a quotation from a medieval
physicist and mystic whose essays on the unknown had struck a

responsive chord. 'One star exists higher than the rest', read the quotation from Paracelsus's *The Hermetic Philosophy.* 'This is the apocalyptic star ... Besides, there is still another star, imagination, which begets a new star and a new heaven'. Varèse insisted that *Arcana* stand as a 'tribute to the author of these words, not a commentary on them'. The work is under twenty minutes long, but its difficulties – for its performers no less than its audience – are daunting. Stokowski later admitted that most of his players detested the piece, as did many hearers. *Musical America's* Oscar Thompson found 'no mercy, no pity in its successions of screaming, clashing, plangorous discords'. It calls for an orchestra of at least 120 players, and keeps them phenomenally busy tracing the unwinding of a single eleven-note theme which undergoes a series of transform-ations and wondrous wide mood-swings.

The conductor and new-music advocate Leopold Stokowski, who conducted several Varèse premières, photographed in 1931

In 1925 Edgard and Louise Varèse bought the house on Sullivan Street, in New York's Greenwich Village, which was to be their home for the rest of their lives. For all the discomfort his music had caused

the more timorous in his audiences, Varèse had found himself a
comfortable station in American musical life. The very outrage of
Hyperprism and *Intégrales* among the chamber works, to say nothing
of the two orchestral works that Stokowski had championed, had
made him something of a legend; his name had become feared, but at
least known. By the late 1920s, however, outrage had gone slightly
out of vogue. Stravinsky's neo-classicism had brought with it a new
passion for the slender, clean sound; Varèse, the most progressive
composer of his time, now faced the possibility of becoming old-
fashioned. Beyond this, the Guild, with its policy of presenting only
brand-new scores, was under attack from rival new-music factions,
particularly the League of Composers, who argued for the establishment of a new-music repertory through regularly scheduled repeat
performances of well-regarded works. The League's official journal,
the influential *Modern Music*, delivered a telling blow, an unsigned
attack on Varèse as being prepared to 'score for a bird-cage, an ash-can
or a carpet sweeper, provided any of these can contribute to his
sonorous whole'. Injured sensibilities were still not sufficiently
soothed when Henry Cowell, in the same publication two years later,
wrote what was surely the first attempt by a serious and qualified
musician to deal with the peculiarities of Varèse's music.

In some anger, Varèse and Salzedo dissolved the Guild in the
autumn of 1927; in its six years it had made New York aware of the
panorama of contemporary creativity the world over through the first
hearings of Arnold Schoenberg's *Pierrot Lunaire*, Igor Stravinsky's
Les Noces, works of Alban Berg, Anton Webern and Paul Hindemith.
Now it was time to move on. The new group was to be called 'The
Pan-American Association of Composers'. Its members, along with
Varèse and Salzedo, included the young Russian conductor Nicolas
Slonimsky, at that time employed as musical secretary to Boston's
Serge Koussevitzky, and the avid experimenter Henry Cowell; even
the reclusive Charles Ives agreed to participate. Varèse stipulated the
group's principles in his usual direct manner. 'The Pan-American
was born because I realized that Europe was drifting back to neo-
classicism … [which] is really academicism, an evil thing for it stifles
spontaneous expression …'

Still obsessed with his search for new tonal resources, Varèse sailed
for France in July 1928 hoping to consult with Parisian sound

engineers 'to do research into certain instruments which we hope will have a voice more in conformity with our age'. Varèse had hoped to establish his own sound laboratory in Paris, but was unable to raise funds. In the city of his birth he was now an unknown quantity. He remedied that situation somewhat by organizing performances of his own music, entirely subsidized by Ives (despite his avowed distaste) under the Pan-American banner.

Edgard and Louise Varèse remained abroad for five years. Gradually his music also crossed the Atlantic. In 1932 Nicolas Slonimsky brought an orchestra to Paris, Berlin and Budapest, and gave those cities their first hearings of some of America's more abstruse new music, including *Arcana* and Charles Ives's *Three Places in New England*, admittedly a heavy dose of contemporary novelty for a single programme. Audiences and the press reacted as expected; 'this tonal monster', one Berlin critic wrote of *Arcana*, 'transforms peaceful concert-goers into wild hyenas'.

In Paris Varèse moved freely once again in that city's artistic milieu – whose members at the time included Stravinsky, hordes of young Americans on their pilgrimages to the classes of Nadia Boulanger, and the ardent advocates of everything under the sun from the new-

Igor Stravinsky, in Paris c. 1930, when he had won acclaim for a wide variety of works from the brutal *Rite of Spring* to the serene *Symphony of Psalms*

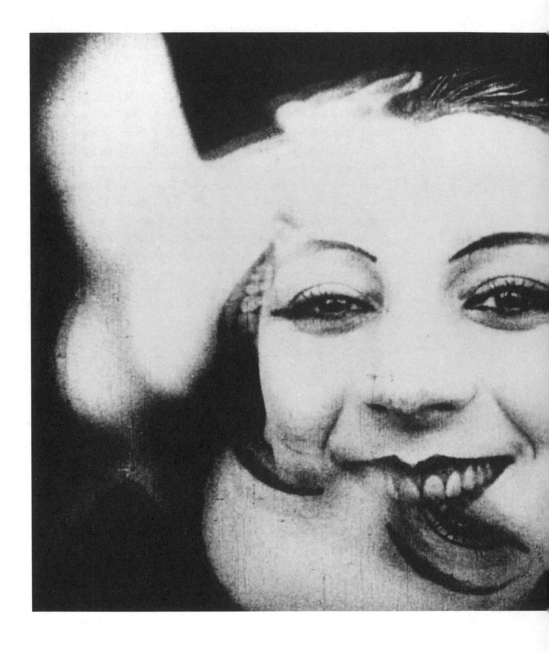

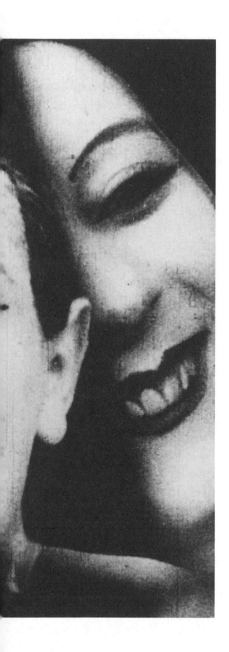

The Cubist, Fernand Léger, created his *Ballet mécanique* in 1924, *left,* to complement George Antheil's score of the same name, a precursor of Varèse's *Ionisation.* In his *Exit the Ballets Russes* of 1914 (now in the Museum of Modern Art, New York), *above,* Léger captured the same innovative spirit that had guided the Russian company's steps in Nijinsky's *The Rite of Spring* the year before.

Conductor and new-music
evangelist Nicolas
Slonimsky, near the time that
he conducted the première
of Varèse's *Ionisation*

fangled jazz to the simplistic 'white music' propounded by Erik Satie.
He worked for a time with Louise on a musical setting of her text on
an American-Indian subject. This came to naught, although some of
the musical ideas found their way into another work that engaged his
ongoing passion for arcane and out-of-reach phenomena. Called
L'Astronome, it was a work set in an observatory, with its central figure
an astronomer who is thrust into space – to the accompaniment of
sirens and aeroplane propellers – to investigate what his telescope had
revealed. The music, Varèse let it be known, was to be 'as strident and
unbearable as possible'. That project, too, was laid to rest before
much had been written.

One other work from Paris, composed in 1933, near the end of
Varèse's stay there, achieved not only completion but quite a degree of
notoriety. The idea of composing a work entirely for an ensemble of
percussion instruments had been in circulation for some time before
Varèse created his *Ionisation*. The gadfly American George Antheil
composed his *Ballet mécanique* in 1926, a musical celebration, complete with eight pianos, siren, propeller and a huge battery of drums,
of the glories of the machine age to accompany an abstract film by
the Cubist, Fernand Léger; it stirred up the expected flurry of interest
and ridicule at its Carnegie Hall première and was soon forgotten.
In 1930 another American, Henry Cowell, began a series of smaller
but more consequential works for percussion.

Ionisation, though only six minutes long, carried the seeds of
musical revolution. Scored for thirty-seven percussion instruments
requiring thirteen players, the work is intensely structured according
to the varying nature of the sonorities involved. Instruments of
definite pitch – celesta, piano and chimes – make their appearance
only near the end, in a kind of apotheosis, played off against the
aggregation of gongs, cymbals and a number of non-Western noisemakers. Like so many other Varèse titles, this one came from the
annals of science – the process of atomic fission. It is said that
scientists many years later, at work on the atomic bomb in Oak
Ridge, Tennessee, listened frequently to the recording of *Ionisation*
made by Nicolas Slonimsky after his presentation of the piece at
Carnegie Hall.

Opposite, the opening
page of the all-percussion
Ionisation, dedicated to
Slonimsky and first performed
under his direction in 1931

Ionisation remains the most popular of Varèse's compositions,
virtually his signature work. Its initial reception, need one add,

to Nicolas Slonimsky

IONISATION

(for Percussion Ensemble of 13 Players)

Edgard Varèse

sounded the familiar chorus of ridicule and denunciation. Even
Slonimsky suffered from the backlash. Engaged to conduct the entire
1933 summer season at the popular Hollywood Bowl in Los Angeles,
he angered audiences from the start with programmes that included
music of Ives, Schoenberg and, worse yet, the notorious *Ionisation*.
The outcry far exceeded the volume of the music itself, and
Slonimsky's contract was annulled soon afterwards.

Varèse returned to New York in time to supervise Slonimsky's
recording of *Ionisation*. Nothing had materialized in his extended
quest for support of his sound experiments; repeated applications for
funding to major American foundations drew continual blanks.
Late in his stay in Paris, Varèse had met Leon Theremin, inventor of
the electronic tone-generator that bears his name. The theremin
did, indeed, produce a continually variable tone, controlled by the
performer's hands in relation to an antenna mounted on an oscillator.
Varèse scored two theremins into his next work, *Ecuatorial*.

Russian-born inventor and
composer Leon Theremin;
the instrument which bore
his name, first demonstrated
in 1920, was one of the
earliest to produce musical
tones by electronic means.

The work was originally scored for solo bass voice, organ, brass and a large percussion contingent; its text comes from an ancient Mayan sacred book, a lament by a tribe lost in a mountainous region; the music, full of outcry and jagged edges of sound, mirrors the 'elemental, rude intensity', as Varèse put it, of the poem. Varèse had hoped to persuade the illustrious Fyodor Shalyapin to undertake the solo part; when that plan did not come to fruition he replaced the single bass with a men's chorus. The theremins proved a disaster at the 1934 première (conducted by the steadfast Slonimsky); they tended to out-wail everything else on stage. Varèse later replaced them with yet another tone-generating device, the ondes martenot of Maurice Martenot, whose wail was more easily controllable through a conventional keyboard.

In the twenty years following *Ecuatorial*, Varèse composed only one brief work, the four-minute flute solo *Density 21.5*, the density of platinum, for the great French flute-player Georges Barrère, who owned an instrument made from that metal. In the intervening years he taught classes in composition and orchestration at the Arsuna School for Fine Arts in Santa Fe, New Mexico, then as now a seductive creative milieu for all the arts. In 1938 Varèse spent some time in Hollywood in a series of vain attempts to convince film producers to finance his sound researches. Back in New York in 1943, he founded the Greater New York Chorus to perform medieval and Renaissance music, which was little known at the time; the group stayed together for four years.

Never in the best of health, Varèse had begun, as early as 1937, to endure fits of profound depression. Friends reported that he would attempt to start a new composition, but would tear up pages as fast as he could fill them. At this time, too, he finally destroyed the manuscript of *Bourgogne*, the ill-fated work of his youth that he had been carrying around with him – as the Ancient Mariner bore his albatross – since the Berlin fiasco. For the most part, these non-productive years were spent in his studio, toying with projects involving explorations into the nature of sound and considering the possibilities that, some day, the world of technology would join the world of music to realize his dreams.

The realities of technology had finally begun to catch up with Varèse's hopes and visions. In 1953 he received the gift of a professional-quality tape recorder, and recognized immediately that he now had at his disposal the means for realizing four decades' worth of dreams. Shortly before, he had begun a work to be called *Déserts*, 'not only physical deserts of sand, sea and mountains', he wrote, 'but also this distant inner space, where man is alone in a world of mystery and essential solitude'. Now he began to record extra material to be fitted in between the instrumental portions of *Déserts*: harsh, grating sounds, some of them recorded in factories, to contrast with the calmer, more spacious instrumental passages. Hermann Scherchen conducted the work's first performance, in 1954 at the Théâtre des Champs Elysées, thus terrorizing yet another audience in the same Paris theatre where Stravinsky's *Rite of Spring* had terrorized its first audiences forty-one years earlier.

Finally, in 1958, Varèse produced the one 'pure' electronic composition that might be said to realize his dream of a music set free from the crippling forces of tonality. For the Philips Pavilion at the Brussels World's Fair, Varèse created the eight-minute *Poème électronique*, entirely on tape, using a collage of studio recordings, altered piano sounds and bells, and filtered recordings of choral music. All of this

Left, Varèse in 1958, editing his first all-electronic composition, the *Poème électronique*, created for the Brussels World's Fair. *Opposite,* the Philips Pavilion at the Brussels World's Fair was co-designed by an architect, Le Corbusier and a composer, Yannis Xenakis.

was encompassed on a three-track tape, created at the Philips studios
at Eindhoven, the Netherlands, with several auditory 'images' fed
through ten amplifiers into a bank of 150 loudspeakers spread through
Le Corbusier's structure so that the music recreated the shape of the
building itself. 'In the *Poème*', said the exultant Varèse, 'I heard my
music – literally in space – for the first time'. Busoni, too, would have
been pleased.

In his final years Varèse produced no music of consequence.
He did, however, enjoy the adulation and honour he had long been
owed. He taught at the famous new-music summer institute at
Darmstadt in 1950. Younger generations of composers, as diverse as
Pierre Boulez and the rock star Frank Zappa (who studied with Varèse
briefly and later anointed himself as apostle) recognized the stature
of his belligerently liberated music and the strength of his visions of
an even greater liberation in time to come.

He was elected to America's National Academy of Arts and Letters
in 1955 and the Royal Swedish Academy in 1962. He received the
Brandeis University Creative Arts Award in 1962, and the first
Koussevitzky International Recording Award in 1963. His music
began to circulate on recordings, in complete editions conducted by
Pierre Boulez and Robert Craft. The house on Sullivan Street offered
a warm welcome to a steadily growing stream of admirers, with
Louise Varèse a gracious hostess and Edgard an outspoken and caustic
critic of anything and everything in the world that had crossed
his path.

Varèse died in New York on 6 November 1965, after surgery for the
removal of an intestinal blockage. In his tribute, Pierre Boulez said,
'Farewell, Varèse, farewell! Your time is finished and now it begins'.

Up until his death, Varèse had been working on *Nocturnal*, a non-
electronic score with a solo soprano intoning verses from Anaïs Nin's
House of Incest and a men's chorus interjecting nonsense syllables.
Nin had visited Varèse at his studio several times around 1940; if not
exactly friends, the two became kindred spirits, their own mystical
visions somehow intertwined. (Nin's diaries, however, mention a visit
in 1941 in which she claims to have seen a tape recorder: a rather
striking prophecy of a technology not yet invented!) The score of
Nocturnal was left unfinished, but was later brought to performable
state by Varèse's pupil, the composer Chou Wen-chung. This work

Opposite, Varèse in the
late 1950s, at home in New
York, where he continued
to inspire musicians as
diverse as Pierre Boulez
and Frank Zappa

aside, Varèse left a legacy of barely a dozen performable scores, less than two hours of music all told.

As the end of the century approached, it became increasingly clear that Varèse – though never part of the mainstream in which the names of Stravinsky, Schoenberg, Bartók and Webern are major landmarks – was the most forward-looking eminence of his time. The concepts he advocated constituted a total revision of the fundamental definition of music. His own definitions were strange and disturbing; he spoke and wrote of music as 'spatial', of 'sound set free yet organized'. Musical form, to him, was a phenomenon of crystallization, the result of a process rather than a mould to be filled. Yet his music moved beyond mere manifesto; brutal, abrasive and, above all, mysterious, it retains the power to seize each listener's imagination and create its own indefinable drama.

4

Henry Cowell, composer, innovator, eloquent defender of the cutting edge in music

American composition up to now has been tied to the apron-strings of European tradition. To attain musical independence, more national consciousness is a present necessity for American composers. The results of such an awakening should be the creation of works capable of being accorded international standing.

Henry Cowell, *American Composers on American Music*, 1933

Henry Cowell

The invited audience at the San Francisco Music Club on 12 March 1912 was beguiled by a piano recital unlike any other in its experience. The pianist was a lad from nearby Menlo Park, named Henry Cowell, performing one day after his fifteenth birthday. The music was his own; the pieces bore such names as *Night Sounds, The Ghouls Gallop* and *Weird Night*, and playing them required the young performer to assault the piano keys with fists and forearms so as to sound several adjacent notes at once (for which he had coined the term 'tone clusters'), and to reach inside the instrument to strum on the strings: techniques now taken for granted among progressive composers, but unheard-of in 1912.

The young man's father, Harry Cowell, had immigrated to California from Ireland via a failed fruit-growing venture in Canada. In San Francisco he married Clarissa Dixon, from a Midwestern farming family; they settled in a small cottage in the foothills above Menlo Park, about twenty miles south of San Francisco. There their son Henry was born (11 March 1897). At five the youngster was on his way to fame as a violin prodigy; a surviving photograph shows the seven-year-old Henry, identified as a pupil of a Doctor Henry Holmes, clutching a full-sized violin, his angelic countenance wreathed in golden curls. But he was soon after overtaken by ill health, a sporadic muscular spasm that was to plague him until early adolescence. He decided, instead, to become a composer, inspired as much as anything by Clarissa Cowell's trove of remembered songs and ballads from her Midwestern upbringing and her Irish forbears. Henry was not to acquire a piano until the age of fourteen:

I was compelled to make my mind into a musical instrument because I had no other, yet desired strongly to hear music frequently. I could not attend enough concerts to satisfy the craving for music, so I formed the habit, when I did attend them, or deliberately rehearsing the compositions I heard and liked, in order that I might play them again mentally whenever I chose.

Aside from a few months' schooling at six, Henry received no formal education. Clarissa and Harry Cowell had divorced when he was eight. Three years later, terrified after San Francisco's catastrophic earthquake, Clarissa and her son had taken to the road, visiting relatives in various towns in the Midwest, ending up in New York, subsisting there for a time on public charities. They returned to Menlo Park in 1910, again living in the shanty in the foothills, where Henry made what money he could as a gardener and a fashioner of wildflower bouquets. By 1912 he had earned enough money to acquire his first piano, a battered upright in lamentable condition but a musical instrument nonetheless.

He had already made some kind of mark. In 1910 he was one of the 'Forty-One Superior Children' singled out by the noted child psychologist Lewis M. Terman, developer of the familiar Intelligence Quotient test (eternally known as the 'IQ'). In his milestone study 'The Intelligence of School Children', Terman's published report on Henry Cowell fills in a remarkable sketch. At fourteen, wrote Terman, his tests revealed a mental age of nineteen:

Although the IQ is satisfactory, it is matched by scores of others among our records, but there is only one Henry … His mother did not see fit to send him to school, nor did she give him much formal instruction at home. She talked with him endlessly, read to him occasionally, and sometimes he read to her … We have a list of over 300 books which Henry had read before he was fourteen years of age, also bulky notes of extensive conversations on such questions as socialism, atheism, scientific problems, etc.

Indeed, it seems clear that Clarissa had played a vital role in shaping her son's outlook on life, in his adolescence and far beyond. She died in 1916; between bouts of illness, she had struggled with a professional writer's career, principally with essays that displayed what we would now identify as a feminist bent. She mixed freely with San Francisco's 'Bohemian' set, among them the writer Jack London. To Henry she preached an austere gospel; sexual relations, he recalled her telling him, were 'absolute wickedness'. She forced him to sever one relationship with a young woman when he was seventeen. Further in the Terman report we read:

*Everybody considered Henry … freakish. If employed to weed a lawn
he was likely to forget what he was doing while trying to compose or
whistle a tune. He had shown promising ability with the violin at the age
of five … but neither violin nor piano was touched again until he was
about fifteen. His musical talent, however, survived all the vicissitudes
of poverty and illness … It remains to be seen whether Henry will
become one of the famous musical composers of his day. Several musical
critics of note hope for this outcome. If he attains fame as a musician,
his biographer is certain to describe his musical genius as natural
and inevitable …*

Terman's predictions proved true in a very short time. The young
Cowell's fame had spread after his first appearance, which the local
press had described in terms fit for a rerun of the 1906 earthquake.
His second public concert – on 5 March 1914, shortly before his
seventeenth birthday, in an elegant ballroom at the Saint Francis
Hotel, sponsored by the San Francisco Musical Society – was well
publicized and drew a large crowd which remained to be startled
by the young pianist–composer's range of pianistic trickery. Cowell
had by then created a vast solo repertory: nearly 100 compositions,
most of them bearing fanciful names (*The Banshee, Fairy Dances,
Message from Mars*, etc.) and most of them demanding some of his
individualistic performance devices. *The Banshee*, a tone picture of the
Gaelic spirit whose wailing foretells imminent death, proved
particularly popular, its wailing achieved by stroking and rubbing
the piano strings; Cowell was later to incorporate this piece into
several other compositions. He had not, furthermore, confined his
explorations into unorthodoxy to the piano. The invention of tone
clusters, he later claimed, was part of his research into resonance and
the nature of harmony, not just a random assault on the keys of the
piano. As early as 1914 he had experimented with new methods of
creating musical structures, including a plan for organizing the serial
sequence of rhythms within a piece which anticipated what other
composers – Pierre Boulez for one – would develop four decades later.

Growing up in San Francisco allowed Cowell access to the panorama of Oriental music maintained by immigrants in that eclectic
city: Chinese and Japanese vocal music, Indonesian gamelans and the
classical music of India. These elements, combined with his mother's

Within ten years after the earthquake and fire, the rebuilt San Francisco was again a teeming metropolis. By then, too, the teenage Henry Cowell had begun to shake up local audiences with his piano inventions.

vivid repertory of American and Irish ballads from her own childhood memories, and the smattering of European symphony and
opera that he could occasionally afford to sample in San Francisco's
music halls, all assured that Cowell would emerge from adolescence
possessed of a musical world view equal in breadth to that of any
living musician. It might even be regarded as beneficial, in fact, that
Cowell's own lack of formal schooling enabled him to assimilate this
wide background without having to filter it through the usual
academic pre-perceptions.

By seventeen, however, Cowell was ready for some outside help in
defining his horizons. Fortunately for his musical predilections, he
was accepted as a student by Charles Seeger, who was at that time
chairman of the music department at the University of California in
nearby Berkeley. Seeger, who virtually invented the study of
musicology as a legitimate pursuit in an American university, was also
one of the few scholars of his time to take a serious interest in non-
Western music. (He would also become the father of the folk-singer
Pete Seeger and the husband, in a second marriage, of the composer
Ruth Crawford Seeger.) Despite Cowell's lack of formal training,
Seeger recognized in the younger man a spirit responsive to his own
interests; he and Cowell were to remain colleagues and collaborators
on several projects throughout their lives.

Seeger saw to it that his free-thinking student received the proper
grounding in harmony and counterpoint without, however, stifling
his freedom to compose as his own conscience dictated. (Compare
this enlightened pedagogy to the academic shackles the Europe-
trained Horatio Parker placed upon Charles Ives, or the conservative
Vincent D'Indy upon Edgard Varèse.) 'Probably his most important
standpoint', Cowell wrote in an 1933 tribute to his mentor, ' is his
advocacy of the intellectual point of view [at a time when] it was
considered that music had value only if it had nothing to do with
the intellect.'

Following his mother's death in 1916, Cowell decided to give
New York a try. He registered for classes at the Institute of Musical
Art, which merely served to expose him to the more stultifying side
of musical academicism; after one term he returned to California.
At Seeger's further urging, he attempted to put into systematic
writing some of the experimental techniques that had captured his

Henry Cowell's *The Banshee*, one of his early works calling for an unusual range of performance techniques. In this piece the pianist runs one hand up and down the strings themselves, while the other hand presses certain notes on the keyboard to reinforce the resonances – all to evoke the howling of Banshees on foggy Irish nights.

imagination. The resulting small book, *New Musical Resources* (completed in 1919 but revised several times before its eventual publication), described in detail not only such Cowell inventions as the tone clusters but also his original ideas on dissonance, shifting rhythms and a whole new theory for the organization of melody and counterpoint according to an original system of ratios.

After a brief stint in the US Army, where he played in bands and also worked as a cook, Cowell tried his luck again in New York, this time as a performer of his own iconoclastic music and as an advocate of the spirit of innovation in the music of others as well. By 1919 he had greatly expanded his repertory of pianistic experiments: not only a gradated variety of tone clusters (involving fists, forearms or wooden boards pressing down on the keys) and invasions into the body of the instrument (strumming or scraping on the strings) but also the notion of placing small foreign objects – bits of paper, nails, screws, etc. – onto the strings to alter the pitch and the sound and to create percussive effects. He had also spread his efforts to other musical forms, creating a pair of quartets – the *Quartet Romantic* for flutes, violin and viola and the *Quartet Euphometric* for strings – whose rhythms were dictated, in Cowell's own intricate calculation methods, by a complex interrelation with the vibration frequencies of the notes and the harmonies. Cowell expressed no hope that either of these works, with their excruciating rhythmic ratios and their dense, non-tonal harmonies, could find performers among the musicians of their time; they were more designed as paradigms of his own musical researches. (They have now been both played and recorded.)

The innovative impulse throbbed in New York in the first years after World War I. The slashing rhythms and tone-colours of the newly-invented jazz inflamed the spirits of composers, and of painters and writers as well. The music of Stravinsky had begun its transatlantic jump; Leopold Stokowski, tireless advocate for the musical last word, had introduced *The Rite of Spring* with his Philadelphia Orchestra in 1922, where one critic heard it as the 'Palaeozoic Crawl'. Edgard Varèse and Carlos Salzedo had begun their well-attended International Composers Guild concerts in 1921; Charles Ives remained an acknowledged if shadowy figure.

On 29 November 1919 Cowell presented himself in his first New York concert, entirely devoted to his own piano works; it attracted

sufficient attention to encourage him to seek professional management for a career as a concert artist. He had, in other words, arrived
on the musical scene in no uncertain terms, with plans to remain.
With his charm and with the added cachet of exoticism in being from
California (where he still maintained the Menlo Park residence) and
being conversant with musical styles beyond the Pacific, Cowell was
welcomed onto the scene. His musical output by 1920 was already
staggering and continued to grow: orchestral works (including one
symphony) full of mysterious harmonies inspired by Irish folk-tales;
vocal works to religious and folkish texts; chamber works ranging
from formal quartets based on Cowell's own invented harmonic
systems to fiddle-tune settings; and literally hundreds of piano works,
from tiny dance pieces to concert-length sonatas and suites. 'To
be both fecund and right', wrote the admiring Virgil Thomson of
Cowell, 'is given to few'.

In 1923 Cowell made the first of many tours of Europe's musical
centres; his piano concerts in Paris, London, Budapest and several
German cities provoked both enthusiasm and outrage. Arnold
Schoenberg invited him to play in his classes in Berlin; Béla Bartók
wrote to ask Cowell's permission, as the presumed inventor of the
tone-cluster, to use the device in some of his own music. Returning
to New York, Cowell gave two formal 'début' recitals, in Carnegie
Hall (4 February 1924) and in Town Hall (17 February); the critical
reception, both for and against, was sensational. Cowell was now an
international celebrity, booked onto the lecture as well as the concert
circuit and for further European appearances.

As tirelessly as he worked on his own career, Cowell also expended
similar energies on behalf of other new music. In 1925 he founded
the New Music Society, initially based in Los Angeles but transferred
a year later to San Francisco; it sponsored concerts of challenging
contemporary music, by both European and American composers,
until its termination in 1936. In 1927 Cowell augmented the activities
of the Society with the quarterly publication *New Music*, devoted
to the publication of new scores – primarily by North and South
American composers, but occasionally by Europeans as well.

It is hard to overestimate the importance of *New Music*, especially
during its first decades when access to the latest worldwide compositional activity was far more sparse than today. Cowell defined the

*Following page left,
programme for the 1924
inaugural concert in a series
at Los Angeles' Biltmore
Hotel, organized by Cowell
and offering brand-new
music from America
and Europe; right, the
programme for three New
York concerts, in the
spring of 1951, by Cowell's
New Music Society, still
true to its original aims.*

The

NEW MUSIC SOCIETY

of

California

(Affiliated with the International Composers' Guild
of New York, Inc.)

Organizer, Henry Cowell
Treasurer, Winifred Hooke

Resident Cooperating Committee
Arthur Bliss, Henry Eichheim, D. Rudhyar

Non-resident Advisory Board
Eugene Goosens, Carl Ruggles, Carlos Salzedo, Edgar Varese

Aim

To present musical works embodying the most progressive
tendencies of this age, and disseminate the new musical ideas

FIRST CONCERT
October 22nd, at 8:15
at the ballroom of the
Biltmore Hotel

with the cooperation of
The Little Symphony, Adolph Tandler directing
Winifred Hooke, Wesley Kuhnle, soloists

Among the works to be performed will be the following:

The Surge of Fire   (symphonic trilogy)   D. Rudhyar
Octandre . . . . Edgar Varese
Angels . . . . Carl Ruggles
Sechs Kleine Klavierstucke . Arnold Shoenberg

(Knabe Pianos)
Tickets for sale ($1.65 tax included) at: Fitzgerald Music Co.—727 So. Hill
Winifred Hooke Studio—462 No. Western Ave.
For reservation by phone call: GRanite 8258 or 7808

NEW MUSIC SOCIETY

PRESENTS 3 CONCERTS

COLUMBIA UNIVERSITY

8:30—MACMILLAN THEATRE

1 MAY 8 ORCHESTRAL CONCERT

MANHATTAN SCHOOL ORCHESTRA
CONDUCTED BY HARRIS DANZIGER
SINFONIETTA—**COWELL**
"LOUSADZAK"—**HOVHANESS**
"OFFRANDES"—**VARESE**
3 MOVEMENTS FOR STRINGS—
WIGGLESWORTH
"LILACS" AND "ANGELS"—**RUGGLES**
ALLELUIA—**HARRISON**
"BEMBE"—**CATURLA**

2 MAY 10 CHAMBER CONCERT

IVES—LARGO, ALLEGRETTO SOMREROSO
LUCK AND WORK
RUSSELL—MARCH SUITE (PERCUSSION)
KOHS—CHAMBER CONCERTO (SOLO)
VIOLA AND STRING NONET.)
THOMSON—"CAPITALS CAPITALS"
TOCH—"FUGE AUS DER GEOGRAPHIE"
GLANVILLE HICKS—HARP SONATA
MCLAREN—SOUND TRACK
NOWAK—SONATA (OBOE AND PIANO)
ARDEVOL—TRIO
BOWLES—"PARLE DETROIT" CANTATA
HARRISON—FUGUE (PERCUSSION)
GOLDMAN—DUO FOR 2 TUBAS
CAGE—IMAGINARY LANDSCAPE
No. 4 (FOR 12 RADIOS)

3 EARLY MUSIC
CHORUS & ORCHESTRA
CONDUCTED BY EDGAR VARESE
DATE TO BE ANNOUNCED

ADMISSION FREE

journal's scope as the publication of 'non-commercial works of artistic value'. If the scores he published were beyond the abilities (or the sympathies) of most performing musicians of the time, it was surely enough that, through Cowell, the names of some of the most significant progressives of the time were at least put into circulation. The first issue contained Carl Ruggles's *Men and Mountains*, pioneering music by a composer virtually unknown at the time; subsequent issues offered music by Ives, Schoenberg, Varèse and Anton Webern. Significant, too, is the fact that, in its 27-year existence, *New Music* published not a single note of music by Cowell himself.

The journal finally brought Cowell face-to-face with the reclusive Ives, to begin a relationship which, with one significant interruption, exerted a powerful enabling force for the growth and health of new American music. Ives lent his support to the publication and to its later offshoot, *New Music Quarterly Recordings*, which Cowell

Henry Cowell, c.1925, demonstrating his 'tone-clusters', in which the pianist smacks down on the keyboard with the entire forearm

The French–American harpist and composer, Carlos Salzedo, was one of Cowell's colleagues in founding the Pan-American Association of Composers in 1928.

Following page, flyers announcing, *left*, the fourth year (1930) of Cowell's influential periodical *New Music* and, *right*, a San Francisco concert in 1932 offering a demonstration of Cowell's newest gadget, the Rhythmicon, developed with the Russian inventor Leon Theremin

launched in 1934. And when Cowell joined Varèse and Salzedo to launch the Pan-American Association of Composers in 1928, Ives again provided considerable financial support for the Association's concerts of American music. Cowell's enthusiasm for Ives's pioneering efforts, throughout his musical career, apparently knew no bounds. 'Public favour comes slowly to those great enough to be independent', Cowell wrote to conclude his essay on Ives in his edited collection *American Composers on American Music*. 'Ives is independent and is truly great; both in invention and in spirit he is one the leading men America has produced in any field.'

Like his fellow pioneer Varèse, Cowell reached a point in his creative existence when the traditional materials available to him began to seem like the mere base of the mountain. His early experiments with tone clusters and his forays into the belly of the pianistic beast were already the symptoms of a need to invent new sounds and

NEW MUSIC

HENRY COWELL ◆ EDITOR

A QUARTERLY PERIODICAL PUBLISHING MODERN MUSIC

NEW MUSIC HAS SUCCESSFULLY COMPLETED ITS THIRD YEAR OF PUBLISHING THE FINEST AMERICAN CONTEMPORARY MUSIC, AND SOME FOREIGN WORKS OF SPECIAL INTEREST, OF A TYPE WHICH GENERAL PUBLISHERS CANNOT HANDLE DUE TO THE LACK OF FINANCIAL SUPPORT. . .

NEW MUSIC IS NONPROFIT MAKING. ANY PROFITS WHICH MAY ACCRUE ARE DIVIDED AMONG THE CONTRIBUTING COMPOSERS. . . . . .

NEW MUSIC HAS BEEN WIDELY REVIEWED THROUGHOUT EUROPE AS WELL AS IN AMERICA, AS BEING THE LEADING PUBLISHER OF MODERN AMERICAN MUSIC. . . . . . .

WE ASK YOU TO HELP SUPPORT THE BEST EXPERIMENTAL AMERICAN MUSIC BY SUBSCRIBING TO NEW MUSIC AT $2.00 PER YEAR. YOU WILL THEN RECEIVE FOUR ISSUES OF MUSIC ALONG NEWER LINES, INCLUDING WORKS FOR PIANO PRIMARILY, AND ALSO ORCHESTRA AND CHAMBER SCORES, SONGS, ETC. . . . . .

THE 1930-31 VOLUME WILL CONTAIN NEW WORKS BY ANTON WEBERN, CARLOS CHAVEZ, ADOLPH WEISS, HENRY BRANT, COLIN McPHEE, ETC.

PLEASE FILL OUT AND RETURN THIS SLIP WITH TWO DOLLARS TO N E W M U S I C , 1950 JONES ST., SAN FRANCISCO, CALIFORNIA, FOR SUBSCRIPTION FOR ONE YEAR. . . . .

NAME .

ADDRESS

The New Music Society

━━━━━ presents ━━━━━

quarter-tone music on two pianos
and a demonstration of the new
musical instrument RHYTHMICON
at the Auditorium of the Y. W. C. A.
620 Sutter Street, San Francisco
Sunday evening, May 15, at 8:15

P R O G R A M

Xanadu — Mildred Couper ━━━━━
(written as incidental music for Eugene
O'Neill's Marco Millions, for two pianos
tuned a quarter tone apart.) Performed
by the composer and Malcolm Thurburn.
Xanadu (repeated) ━━━━━

Demonstration by Henry Cowell

of his new instrument
the COWELL-THEREMIN RHYTHMICON

━━━━━

The rhythmicon is a new musical instrument
for the production of rhythms of all types
by the holding of keys on the keyboard. As
long as the key is held, the corresponding
rhythm will be sustained. Rhythmic harmonies produced by sounding several rhythms
together are made easy and practical to
perform. The rhythm is related to sound
scientifically, so that a sonal harmony corresponding to the rhythm in vibration ratio
is always heard. The sound and rhythm are
both produced by a new principle of television, and are caused by the influence of
light on a photo-electric cell. ━━━━━

Public admission, one dollar.
(New Music Society members free on presentation of membership cards.) ━━━━━

new ways of using them. Now, in the late 1920s, he began to look
further. He plunged voraciously into the worldwide realm of music
past and present. Early American music, the hymnodies of
the eighteenth-century New England choir-masters, constituted one
thrilling discovery; he fashioned contemporary settings of some of the
Fuguing Tunes of Boston's William Billings. Oriental music provided
another source of fascination; he studied the Indonesian gamelan
with a Javanese musician, and learned to play the Japanese flute, the
shakuhachi. Charles Seeger had taught him that music had no
boundaries; in the prime of his creative existence, Cowell put those
teachings to gainful employment.

He still dreamed of a musical resource that would allow performances of the complex rhythmic patterns that he had so far only
been able to theorize. One pathway led him to Leon Theremin, the

The aim of *New Music* was
to publish not only news
about new scores but also
the scores themselves. The
first issue, October 1927,
left, contained Carl Ruggles'
Men and Mountains of
1924, *right,* which Ruggles
had originally published
privately, to little circulation.

TO MY FRIEND

EUGENE   SCHOEN

" GREAT THINGS ARE DONE WHEN MEN AND
MOUNTAINS MEET "

Blake

SYMPHONIC   ENSEMBLE

MEN AND MOUNTAINS

CARL   RUGGLES

CR

ARLINGTON, VERMONT
1924

Russian-born sound engineer and inventor, the wail of whose epony-
mous instrument had fascinated Varèse for a time. Out of their
consultations came the Rhythmicon, unleashed at a demonstration
concert at New York's New School for Social Research on 19 January
1932. Giving off a sound similar to a reed organ, and operated
through a sixteen-note keyboard, with each key defining a distinct
and complex rhythmic pattern, Theremin's instrument consisted of a
series of rotating wheels which interrupted beams of light to produce
its patterns with astonishing accuracy. Cowell composed two major
works for the instrument: *Rhythmicana*, which pitted it against an
orchestration devised by Nicolas Slonimsky, and Music for Violin and
Rhythmicon. The experiment proved a dead end; Theremin's box
was later used in psychological research, but not in music.

At the height of his fame, however, Cowell's career reached an
unexpected, and momentarily disabling juncture. Back at his Menlo
Park cottage, Cowell had long enjoyed an easy-going friendship with
his neighbours, including teenage boys whom he allowed to swim in
his pond. In the spring of 1936 the Menlo Park police – spurred by
long-standing rumours that Cowell regularly consorted with artists,
authors, musicians and other assorted 'Bohemians', and that he must
also, therefore, be a Communist – investigated reports that boys were
'running wild' at the homestead. On the testimony of one seventeen-
year-old boy, who had unsucessfully attempted to blackmail him,
Cowell was arrested as a homosexual. Naive and trusting as he was
throughout his life, Cowell initially saw no need to hire a defence
attorney, and was persuaded to do so only after the intervention of
Harry Cowell and his second wife Olive. From his cell he composed
a full confession, along with a plea for leniency on the grounds that
he would be of greater value to the world outside than in prison.
Harry Cowell tried to plead with the authorities, promising to remove
Henry from the area, even from the country if necessary, but the
strength of the confession outweighed their pleas. Henry received the
maximum sentence of fifteen years, in the California State Prison at
San Quentin.

It might have been understandable if the harsh and, arguably,
unjust decision by the California courts had ended the career of the
man whom the critic Alfred Frankenstein identified as 'the central
figure in the American musical avant garde'. Cowell, however, proved

himself made of sterner stuff. Determined to transcend, by whatever means, his sordid surroundings, he applied himself with new vigour to his music. He composed in his cell, including a piece for band based on the moods and personalities of other inmates he had observed. At one of the prison's monthly 'vaudeville' nights he played some of his own music on a battered piano and earned an ovation.

Before long, in fact, Cowell found himself as immersed in music inside prison walls as he had ever been outside. The prison's bandmaster, John Hendricks (himself a convicted killer) arranged for

Upon his sentencing to fifteen years at San Quentin Prison, Cowell suffered the further indignity of the prison number and mug-shot.

Cowell to become his assistant, and Cowell entered happily on a career as band conductor, teacher of musicianship to about 200 students a day, composer, arranger and copyist for both prison and outside ensembles. In his band concerts he introduced a discreet amount of serious music and was gratified at the response. 'There are some [prisoners] who do not enjoy "classical" music,' he wrote to a friend, 'but among those who do there is a preference for a rather severe programme, and we do not dare to put on what they consider compromises'. He nurtured an old friendship with the ethnomusicologist (Miss) Sidney Robertson, who became, along with Slonimsky, the principal conduit for information from, to and about Cowell – and who was to become, soon after Cowell's release, his wife and valued collaborator.

There were also discoveries to be made by Cowell himself, in the form of the music favoured by the prison's ethnic groups. Mandolins and guitars, he wrote, vastly outnumbered concert instruments; he heard Serbian tamburitza ensembles and Ozark fiddlers. By 1939 Cowell was teaching music full-time in a thriving music school with nearly 2,000 registrations. He formed a prison orchestra and a series of chamber-music concerts. All told, his musical work at San Quentin – vividly demonstrating the superior value of rehabilitation over punishment – greatly influenced a change in the attitudes of penal officials throughout America.

Meanwhile, the musical world – though not all of it – rallied to Cowell's defence. To Cowell's great distress, both Charles and Harmony Ives broke off all contact, refused to answer any of Cowell's letters or discuss the matter. By the light of Ives's rockbound Yankee moral standards, Henry Cowell had suddenly become a non-person. (He would regain his status in Ives's estimation just as suddenly when, after release, he found himself a wife.) Carl Ruggles briefly broke ties with Cowell; so did the composer Ernst Bacon – 'to my considerable shame', he later admitted. Both soon relented. Edgard Varèse visited Cowell in prison, and vainly attempted a personal plea to officials on his behalf. Lewis Terman, who had first dealt with the thirteen-year-old Cowell as a case study in precocious intelligence, interviewed Cowell in prison and determined that the 39-year-old prisoner was 'not a true homosexual, but was merely delayed in his heterosexual adjustment due to the feminine influences about him during his childhood'.

The eccentric composer-pianist Percy Grainger helped facilitate Cowell's early release from prison by offering him employment as his musical assistant.

The most vociferous of Cowell's defenders was himself something of an eccentric: the Australia-born American pianist, composer and blithe spirit Percy Grainger, then living in New York. He wrote to Olive Cowell that her stepson was a man 'wholly good and incapable of evil'. 'I know in advance', he continued, 'that when he & mankind or he & the law are in disagreement that Henry Cowell is right & the others are wrong'.

In October 1939 Grainger wrote to the prison board, offering to employ Cowell as a live-in research assistant if he were granted parole. With a new governor in the California State House and his own exemplary prison record, Cowell won his parole and moved to Grainger's house outside New York City in June 1940. Almost immediately his musical career regained momentum as if the four-year hiatus had never existed. In the first four months of 1941, for example, he conducted two orchestral programmes with the New York Civic Symphony, served as commentator for a broadcast of American music, gave two recitals, judged a composition contest, supervised seven performances of his own works, composed or arranged eight others, wrote five articles and taught at three New York schools. Later that year, on 27 September 1941, he and Sidney Robertson were married. Charles Ives sent a personal letter of congratulation, and the two old friends were reunited in person on 14 April 1942, resuming their collaboration as before. Over some lightly phrased protest – Harmony Ives confessed that she hated seeing her name in print – the Cowells began a jointly written biography of Ives; its final words were dated 15 May 1954, four days before Ives's death.

Over and above these activities, Cowell fell into another position that would underscore his value to society, which he and his close friends had always tried to proclaim. In December 1940 the United States Government organized a programme to be called 'Cultural Defence', whose primary purpose was to defeat recent German propaganda aimed at stirring up enmity between the USA and Latin-American countries. Cowell, his civil rights restored by the California prison board so that he could now work for the Government, signed on as an authority on Latin-American music, responsible for the two way routing of scores between the USA and Latin countries. The benevolent Charles Seeger wrote to California's governor, calling his attention to Cowell's work in this music exchange, and urging him to consider a full and unconditional pardon so that Cowell could further enhance his work on behalf of the war effort. With mere days left in his term, on 28 December 1942, Governor Culbert Olson granted the pardon. Soon thereafter Cowell became Senior Music Editor for the overseas branch of the Office of War Information.

Cowell was then forty-five. Behind him lay a legacy of nearly 700 separate compositions, as listed chronologically in William Lichtenwanger's *The Music of Henry Cowell*, A Descriptive Catalog. They constitute a panorama of musical adventure and experimentation. The piano music, with its vast expansion of that instrument's resources, offered a range of tone colour unheard of in the works of any previous composer; not even Franz Liszt, with his power to turn his piano into some kind of virtuoso super-orchestra, approached the

Opposite, fully restored to respectability, Cowell resumed his services on behalf of new music.

tonal spectrum that Cowell achieved in such early works as *The Banshee*, with its wailing as if from the far side of the moon, or *The Tides of Manaunaun*, with its pounding tone clusters like the roar of waves against a Celtic shore. Other music reached towards even further timbral horizons: the 1924 work called, simply, *Ensemble*, which proposed the ecumenical combination of a string quartet and the 'thunder sticks' of the indigenous peoples of the American Southwest; the 1934 *Ostinato pianissimo*, moving forward with beautiful subtlety from Varèse's conception of music composed entirely for percussion ensemble. In even more subtle ways, much of Cowell's music proposed abstruse structural organization: rhythmic outlines derived from harmonic resonances or, in the 1936 'Mosaic' Quartet, the players set free to choose the order of events in the music by piecing together on their own a series of unconnected given passages. If any of this sounds like the later experiments of, say, Pierre Boulez or Karlheinz Stockhausen, bear in mind that Cowell came first.

The American self-exile Conlon Nancarrow, living in Mexico City since 1940, is one of the most successful composers to follow Cowell's example in broadening the scope of what the piano can accomplish. He composes for player-piano, punching the paper piano rolls by hand and thus achieving an amazing complexity of rhythm and counterpoint.

The four years in prison constituted a break in Cowell's chronology; they seem to have formed a kind of boundary line in his music as well. Most of his music from 1942 and until his death in 1965 – another 250 entries in the Lichtenwanger catalogue – seemed to abandon the old experimental stance, as though Cowell imagined that his points along that line had already been made. The music became simpler, the rhythms more straightforward, the harmonies no longer forbidding. He completed no fewer than seventeen symphonies in those years (and partially completed two more); they are attractive, short pieces, drawing upon folk or folk-like materials, breaking out now and then into a jig that Clarissa Cowell might be said to smile down upon. There were dozens of short pieces for piano or violin, many of them bearing affectionate, domestic titles like *Love to Sidney*. By far the strongest of the late works stemmed from his continuing fascination with Asian music: India in his 'Madras' Symphony; Iran in his *Persian Set*; Japan in his *Ongaku* and two concertos for koto and orchestra.

If his own innovative juices may have cooled slightly in those last years, his zeal on behalf of the contemporary creative scene certainly did not. He resumed his classes at the ultra-progressive New School for Social Research, expounding on new music, inviting other composers in for his students to 'meet', and lecturing as well on the music of other cultures. He also taught at Columbia University and Baltimore's Peabody Conservatory. Among his pupils were George Gershwin and Burt Bacharach (briefly) and, more importantly, John Cage and Lou Harrison. It was from Cowell that Cage absorbed the idea of 'preparing' a piano by introducing items of hardware onto the strings; from Cowell, too, came Lou Harrison's ambitions to incorporate music of Pacific lands into his own musical style. And it was also from Cowell that these composers – along with countless others of their generation and other generations since – gleaned the idea that new music could flourish free of preconceptions and restraints, beholden only to the conscience of its creator.

In the way the world tends to regard greatness, it may be difficult to apply that epithet to Cowell's music. Beyond question, each of the experimental early works, the piano pieces in particular, came first to life as a cleverly conceived gadget: it was the experiment that was of prime importance, not the communicative power of the result.

Cowell thrived on the act of combination: a tune for violin singing
prettily over a wild and wonderful assortment of Indonesian
percussion and gongs doing something entirely different. Yet that
very act (in a 1952 work called *Set of Five*) defines both the eclectic
genius of Cowell himself and the polyglot nature of his America.

Every one of his musical inventions has had its contemporary
resonance. We may smile tolerantly at Cowell's involvement with the
pretensions of Dr Theremin's Rhythmicon, with its power to
combine wildly divergent rhythmic patterns. Yet the composer
Conlon Nancarrow devotes his energies to yet another device for
securing the same astonishing complexity; he does it by hand,
punching holes in rolls of paper that activate a player-piano. The

Henry Cowell and his
favourite musical assistant,
hard at work

Scots-Armenian-American Alan Hovhaness has attempted a similar mixture of primitive American tune-smithing with non-Western materials.

If not a great composer himself, Cowell has been one of the strongest seminal influences on the course of American music. Perhaps what he created was art, perhaps it was merely the material out of which art might be made. Its importance cannot be denied, nor its vigour.

5

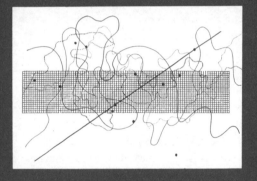

John Cage's score for
Fantasa Mix, composed
in 1958

*There is no such thing as an empty space or an
empty time. There is always something to see,
something to hear. In fact, try as we may to
make a silence, we cannot. Sounds occur
whether intended or not. One must see that
humanity and nature, not separate, are in this
world together; that nothing was lost when
everything was given away.*

John Cage, *Silence,* 1973

John Cage

For several months before his death (of a stroke in his New York apartment on 12 August 1992) John Cage had been working with curators at the Los Angeles Museum of Contemporary Art, fashioning an extensive exhibition in which he was to be the central figure. Cage had chosen the title, *Rolywholyover   A Circus*; it came from one of his favourite texts, James Joyce's *Finnegans Wake*; just the sound of the word seemed to signalize a fine and rowdy celebration. The show, which finally opened in September 1993, drew large crowds and was then transported to museums in several other American cities; it truly embraced the totality of John Cage, the range of his visions and interests, and the joy he derived from them. There were showcases that celebrated his passion for collecting wild mushrooms and fashioning original macrobiotic recipes from them; others that honoured his love of game-playing and puzzles. His own paintings adorned the walls of one room; another even larger room was hung with the works of artists he knew and cherished, among them Jasper Johns, Marcel Duchamp, Morris Graves and Robert Rauschenberg. There were tables with chessboards at which visitors were invited to play; cupboards crammed with pictures, manuscripts, old books, a computer or two on which visitors were presented with bits of text and music and invited to share their own compositions. Most important, the actual content of the show changed every day: some pieces taken down, others put up, the exact selection and arrangement of objects determined by the museum staff through a daily consultation with *I Ching*, the ancient Chinese oracle that had guided much of Cage's activity during his lifetime, and that continued to do so in his absence. The catalogue for the show consisted of a metal box filled with papers of various sizes: essays, prints, photographs, a serendipity to match the exhibit itself. Cage had hoped that the contents of the catalogue could also be changed every day, but museum officials had convinced him of the impracticality of that.

Few museum displays had ever captured so much of the creative energy and personal warmth of a chosen artist. No visitor, whether

Rolywholyover   A Circus was the vast, constantly changeable tribute to John Cage mounted by the Los Angeles Museum of Contemporary Art in 1993. This is the invitation to its preview, showing river rocks as used by Cage in his *Watercolour Workshop,* 1988.

one-time intimate of Cage or total stranger, could have failed to feel his presence in those museum rooms: the childlike smile, the soft and gentle voice (even when stipulating some new experimental outrage), the eagerness to reach out towards a far horizon where all the arts come together in a single, gloriously eclectic language.

In 1986 the California Institute of the Arts, the experimental artistic hotbed founded through funds bequeathed by, of all unlikely sources, the late Walt Disney, had awarded Cage the honorary degree of 'Doctor of All the Arts'. To approach the importance of John Cage from the single criterion of 'composer' is to miss the astonishing breadth of his visions and their impact on the cultural world. In its entire history, after all, the Los Angeles Philharmonic – with its headquarters only a block away from the Museum – had played only a single work of Cage (and stirred up a riot of protest in the audience on that one occasion); if this seems like cavalier treatment of the native son of Los Angeles who earned recognition as one of the most innovative forces of his day, the musical establishments in most other major American cities had done little better on Cage's behalf. Rather than a formal concert hall, the broad expanses of a museum's exhibition hall seemed the more appropriate place to celebrate his multi-layered genius.

It is also significant that the most famous of Cage's musical compositions happens to be a piece in which the performer (usually, but not necessarily, a solo pianist) assumes a playing position, turns pages at specific times, observes breaks between the three movements, stands up to take a bow at the end, but for the entire four-minutes and thirty-three seconds of the work draws no sound from the instrument. Typically, Cage drew the inspiration for *4'33"*, as the work is known, from the visual arts: from the series of 'white' paintings by his friend and sometime colleague Robert Rauschenberg. As Rauschenberg postulated the dynamic of his paintings as their reaction to the changing light in the rooms in which they might be hung, and the conditions created by people coming and going in those rooms, so Cage conceived *4'33"*, as a piece of music constantly in flux, subject to the ambient sounds surrounding each performance.

Of all Cage's prodigal musical output (more than 200 separate compositions, most of them published) *4'33"* remains 'the pivotal composition of this century', as the record producer John McClure once proclaimed. Cage himself remained reverential towards it. 'Not a day goes by', he asserted, 'without my making use of that piece in my life and work. I always think about it before I write my next piece.'

Arnold Schoenberg, whose composition classes in Los Angeles Cage attended briefly in 1934, informed his 22-year-old student that he was not really a composer at all, but an inventor. That comment seems to have pleased Cage; Schoenberg's words accorded him close kinship with two of his particular idols, who also happened to be inventors. One was his father, John Milton Cage senior, a flourishing inventor with a particular interest in undersea vessels; one of his devices successfully detected German submarines in the English Channel during World War I. The other was the archetypal American rebel Henry David Thoreau, who in his early days, while working in his father's factory, had designed a device for the easier manufacture of lead pencils.

John Milton Cage senior grew up in Greeley, Colorado, the rebellious son of a Baptist missionary who had preached that music was the work of the devil. He married Lucretia Harvey, pianist at a local church; she, too, was something of a rebel, given to the practice, forbidden by her family, of reading books. The young couple fled the restricting atmosphere of Colorado church life and settled in Los Angeles, where their only surviving child, John junior – two previous sons had died in infancy – was born on 5 September 1912. The boy

Above, three generations: Gustavus Adolphus Williamson Cage, his son John Milton Cage Sr., and grandson John Milton Cage Jr., in Colorado, 1916
Left, Lucretia (Crete) Harvey, mother of John Cage: her reputation as a rebel was based on her propensity for reading books.

displayed a lively interest in the intelligent world around him; at eight
he had begun piano lessons with an aunt and expressed a fondness
for the music of Edvard Grieg. At fifteen he won a student oratorical
contest, delivering in the vast outdoor spaces of the Hollywood
Bowl a speech entitled *Other People Think*, a plea for recognition by
Americans of the ideals and achievements of foreign cultures. He
thought well enough of that speech to deliver it again, sixty years
later, at celebrations of his seventy-fifth birthday.

By the age of twenty Cage had cultivated his powers of self-
expression in several fields. After high school he entered Pomona
College, first intending to study for the ministry, later shifting his
horizons towards writing, but he dropped out after two years. During
two years of European wandering, financed by an allowance from his
parents, he dabbled in painting and architecture, wrote poetry and,
under the spell of Majorcan skies, attempted his first musical creations,
now lost – 'composed in some mathematical way I no longer recall', as
he described them in an Autobiographical Note of 1989.

Returning to California late in 1931, Cage supported himself by
working as a gardener at a Santa Monica motel, and by lecturing on
modern painting and music to housewives. He studied for a time
with the Chicago-born pianist and teacher Richard Buhlig, 'a wonderful, cultivated man [who] taught me a great deal', he later remembered. Buhlig was something of a cult figure in Los Angeles circles,
known for the austere strength of his Beethoven and new-music
performances. Ostensibly, he taught piano, but he also looked over
some of Cage's early compositions and pointed out what would and
would not work. Buhlig had also taught Henry Cowell, and brought
the two composers together. Cowell urged Cage to take his classes
in contemporary composition and non-Western music at the New
School for Social Research in New York. Cage moved to New York
in 1933, and studied with Cowell for a year.

Back in California, he began private lessons with Arnold
Schoenberg in autumn 1934, under what seems to have been a continuous cloud of protest on both sides. 'It became clear to the both of
us', Cage wrote, 'that I had no feeling for harmony. Therefore, he
said, I'd never be able to write music. "Why not?" "You'll come to a
wall and won't be able to get through". "Then I'll spend my life
knocking my head against that wall".' Undaunted, Cage began to

Austrian refugee composer
Arnold Schoenberg, *right*,
told the young John Cage,
below, that he was more
an inventor than a
composer. Cage took this
as a compliment.

compose in earnest, using an organizational method that somewhat resembled Schoenberg's twelve-note system but that imposed even more stringent rules. Cage's system employed not Schoenberg's twelve but the twenty-five notes of two successive chromatic octaves, with the stricture that no note could be repeated until all twenty-five had been played – a curious turn in his musical philosophy considering the artistic freedoms embodied in later works. In 1934, too, while working behind the counter of his mother's art-goods shop, Cage fell in love-at-first-sight with an attractive customer, Xenia Andreyevna Kashevaroff, born in Alaska of Russian parentage. He proposed marriage on the spot; she accepted with minimal hesitation. The marriage endured eleven years.

In 1936 the film-maker Oscar Fischinger invited Cage to compose the music for one of his projects. In the early days of sound films, Fischinger had created a number of abstract filmic treatments of well-known classical compositions, and he is best remembered today for the 'Toccata and Fugue' sequence in Walt Disney's *Fantasia*. Meeting Cage gave Fischinger the idea of using original new scores created hand-in-hand with the visual imagery. Although none of their collaborations reached fruition, one comment by Fischinger stirred a particular response in Cage. 'Everything in the world has its own spirit,' Cage remembered him saying, 'which can be released by setting it into vibration'. Immediately, Cage set upon an organized exploration of the vibration potential of familiar objects. 'I began hitting, rubbing everything, listening and then creating percussion music, and playing it with friends.' Xenia Cage was a bookbinder by trade; she and her new husband lived in a communal house with several other bookbinders, and they became the 'orchestra' for Cage's first percussion pieces. One surviving work from those informal sessions, a trio for some of the quieter members of the percussion family (bamboo sticks, pieces of wood of various sizes, etc.) can be reckoned the true start of Cage's career as an experimental composer.

Clearly, the inventive spirit of John Milton Cage senior had migrated to his son as well. At Cowell's suggestion, Cage took to exploring junkyards, acquiring a trove of discarded brake drums, tram-car springs and metal sheets, each piece a source of splendid percussive sounds. The notion of creating music solely for percussion ensemble had already gained some notoriety, through the 1925 *Ballet mécanique* of George Antheil and, more important, Edgard Varèse's *Ionisation* of 1933, which was now available on a recording conducted by Nicolas Slonimsky. Cage, however, delved even further into the potential of the new medium. Exact musical pitches were, of course, not possible in an ensemble of banged-upon brake drums and similar noisemakers; musical structure based on melody and harmony, the binding force of Western music from Renaissance polyphony to Schoenberg's note-rows, was outside the realm of these new musical sounds. In their place Cage – who had already confessed to Schoenberg, after all, that he had no feeling for harmony – devised an intricate system for imparting formal logic to a work through an exactly controlled sequence of additive rhythmic patterns. 'This rhythmic structure', he wrote, 'could be expressed with any sounds, including noise … or as stillness'. One of his first percussion works, for example, consisted of sixteen repetitions of a pattern of 4+3+2+3+4 beats. Cage had bravely invited Schoenberg to visit one of the percussion evenings with the bookbinders; Schoenberg responded that he had no intention of being free for such a visit 'now or at any time'.

In 1938 Cage accepted a position as pianist and resident composer for dance classes at the small, progressive Cornish School in Seattle. There he met a promising young dancer, seven years his junior, named Merce Cunningham, whose views on innovation and creativity he found congenial; they formed a productive partnership that was to last a lifetime. A progressive school founded on the belief that all arts students should be prepared to experience all the arts, Cornish attracted some of the leading figures in many areas of artistic activity, among them the painters Mark Tobey and Morris Graves. No phase of human thought escaped the collective concern of this unique gathering – the teachings of Zen Buddhism, for example (which Cage first encountered at Cornish in a lecture by his colleague Nancy Wilson Ross), that he would later explore even further and 'which took the place for me of psychoanalysis'. From his first readings in Zen, Cage made a number of life-preserving decisions: that music is meant to quiet the mind, making it susceptible to divine influences, and that the responsibility of the artist is to imitate nature in her manner of operation.

For a dance piece at Cornish, on an African theme, Cage was asked to provide appropriate music. The auditorium had no orchestral pit;

Dancer/choreographer
Merce Cunningham (right)
lived and collaborated
with Cage from the time of
their meeting in 1938
until Cage's death fifty-four
years later.

Cage had the idea he had previously heard demonstrated in some
of Henry Cowell's atmospheric pieces, of 'preparing' the piano by
imposing small foreign objects – nails, screws, various pieces of
hardware, feathers – onto or between the strings of a grand piano,
thus cancelling out the exact pitch of a string and producing a hazy,
pitchless percussive sound – a cross, perhaps, between an out-of-tune
harpsichord and an Indonesian gamelan. This proved to be the
second of Cage's major inventions, as fraught with potential as were
his earlier works for percussion ensemble. In 1940 he composed his
first significant prepared-piano work, a *Bacchanale* to accompany a

A typical Cageian 'prepared
piano', with screws, bolts
and hardware placed at
carefully determined spots
on the strings to create a
kaleidoscope of new sounds

dance creation. He continued his explorations into the potential
of percussion-ensemble writing, joining forces with another
Cowell protégé, Lou Harrison, for a series of percussion concerts
in San Francisco.

Bearing in mind Cage's later reputation as an unruly iconoclast,
the prepared-piano pieces may come as a comforting surprise. The
sounds they most immediately evoke are those of the Indonesian
gamelan: gentle, repetitive music a little like the patterns of batik
fabric prints on the one hand, and reminiscent of Debussy's Orient-
inspired piano music on the other. 'The prepared piano ...' he later
wrote, 'led me to the enjoyment of things as they come, rather than
as they are kept, or possessed, or forced to be'.

His time at Cornish left Cage facing horizons greatly expanded.
Merce Cunningham, Mark Tobey and Morris Graves had helped
shape those horizons, and led Cage to recognize a hitherto unsus-
pected closeness among the expressive arts. That knowledge, with his
passionate discovery of the teachings of the Zen masters, greatly
deepened his outlook on his own work. The invention of the 'prepared' piano suggested new sound possibilities. So did the student
operators at the Cornish School radio station, who initiated Cage into
yet another realm of sonic possibilities, the mingling of acoustic and
amplified sounds, along with sine-wave recordings, forerunner of an
electronic era still to come.

Assisting his father in his submarine researches, deemed vital to the
war effort, earned Cage exemption from the draft. In 1942 he moved
his base of operations to New York. Merce Cunningham was in New
York as well; after a time as a dancer with Martha Graham's brilliant
young company he had begun to present his own choreography, with
Cage providing most of the music. Both Cunningham and Cage
approached the process of combining music and movement from an
innovative point of view; the two elements, they proclaimed, should
function independent of each other. Such a concept demanded
a particular degree of strength in a dancer, capable of maintaining a
fluidity of movement even when the pulse of the music became
a contradictory force. In 1944 Cunningham formed his own
company, with Cage as music director – a position he was to hold
until 1966 – and began giving concerts in and out of New York,
to considerable acclaim.

*Opposite, the 'score'
for Cage's Sonatas and
Interludes, detailing the
exact placement of each
piece of hardware along the
piano's sounding board*

TONE

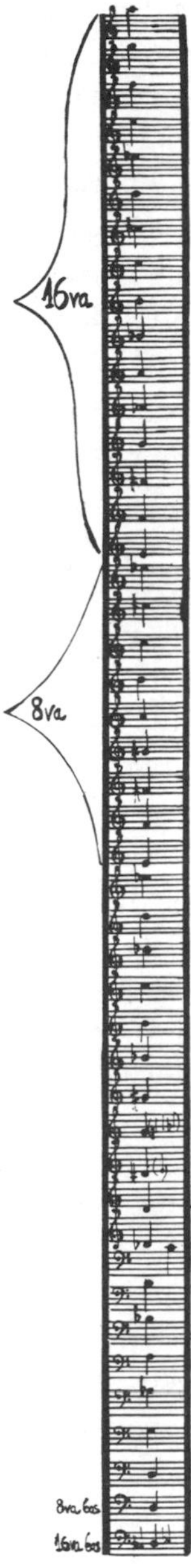

MATERIAL	STRINGS LEFT TO RIGHT	DISTANCE FROM DAMPER (INCHES)	MATERIAL	STRINGS LEFT TO RIGHT	DISTANCE FROM DAMPER (INCHES)	MATERIAL	STRINGS LEFT TO RIGHT	DISTANCE FROM DAMPER (INCHES)	TONE
			SCREW	2-3	1 1/4 *				A
			MED. BOLT	2-3	1 3/8 *				G
			SCREW	2-3	1 5/8 *				F
			SCREW	2-3	1 13/16 *				E
			SCREW	2-3	1 3/4 *				E♭
			SM. BOLT	2-3	2 *				D
			SCREW	2-3	1 9/16 *				C♯
			FURNITURE BOLT	2-3	2 3/16 *				C
			SCREW	2-3	2 1/2 *				B
			SCREW	2-3	1 7/8 *				B♭
			MED. BOLT	2-3	2 7/8 *				A
			SCREW	2-3	2 1/4 *				A♭
			SCREW	2-3	3 3/4 *				G
			SCREW	2-3	2 15/16 *				F♯
SCREW	1-2	3/4 *	FURN. BOLT + 2 NUTS	2-3	2 1/8 *	SCREW + 2 NUTS	2-3	3 1/4 *	F
			SCREW	2-3	1 13/16 *				E
			FURNITURE BOLT	2-3	1 7/8				E♭
			SCREW	2-3	1 15/16				C♯
			SCREW	2-3	1 1/16				C
(DAMPER TO BRIDGE = 4 7/16; ADJUST ACCORDINGLY)			MED. BOLT	2-3	3 3/4				B
			SCREW	2-3	4 7/16				A
RUBBER	1-2-3	4 1/2	FURNITURE BOLT	2-3	1 1/4				G♯
			SCREW	2-3	1 3/4				F♯
			SCREW	2-3	2 5/16				F
RUBBER	1-2-3	5 3/4							E
RUBBER	1-2-3	6 1/2	FURN. BOLT + NUT	2-3	6 7/8				E♭
			FURNITURE BOLT	2-3	2 9/16				D
RUBBER	1-2-3	3 5/8							D♭
			BOLT	2-3	7 1/8				C
			BOLT	2-3	2				B
SCREW	1-2	10	SCREW	2-3	1	RUBBER	1-2-3	8 1/4	B♭
(PLASTIC (See G))	1-2-3	2 5/16				RUBBER	1-2-3	4 1/2	G♯
PLASTIC (OVER 1 - UNDER 2-3)	1-2-3	2 7/8				RUBBER	1-2-3	10 1/8	G
(PLASTIC (See D))	1-2-3	4 1/4				RUBBER	1-2-3	5 7/16	D♯
PLASTIC (OVER 1 - UNDER 2-3)	1-2-3	4 1/8				RUBBER	1-2-3	9 3/4	D
BOLT	1-2	15 1/2	BOLT	2-3	11/16	RUBBER	1-2-3	14 1/8	D♭
BOLT	1-2	14 1/2	BOLT	2-3	7/8	RUBBER	1-2-3	6 1/2	C
BOLT	1-2	14 3/4	BOLT	2-3	9/16	RUBBER	1-2-3	14	B
RUBBER	1-2-3	9 1/2	MED. BOLT	2-3	10 1/8				B♭
SCREW	1-2	5 7/8	LG. BOLT	2-3	5 7/8	SCREW + NUTS	1-2	1	A
BOLT	1-2	7 1/8	MED. BOLT	2-3	2 1/4	RUBBER	1-2-3	4 1/8	A♭
LONG BOLT	1-2	8 3/4	LG BOLT	2-3	3 1/4				G
			BOLT	2-3	11/16				D
SCREW + RUBBER	1-2	4 9/16							D
ERASER (OVER D UNDER C♯ + E♭) AM. PENCIL CO. #346	1	6 3/4							D

* MEASURE FROM BRIDGE.

By the mid-1940s both Cage and Cunningham had become recognized among New York's major revolutionary forces. Their widen-
ing circle of intimates included such illustrious figures as the surrealist
painter and novelist Max Ernst, the patron Peggy Guggenheim, the
composer–critic Virgil Thomson and the poet Kenneth Patchen
(with whom Cage created a radio play for the Columbia Broadcasting
System entitled *The City Wears a Slouch Hat*). A programme at the
Museum of Modern Art in February 1943 was the first in a series of
concerts and recitals that established Cage's reputation as both hero
and irritant on the New York avant-garde scene; the programme
included the *First Construction* for percussion ensemble, *Imaginary
Landscape No.1* for percussion plus recordings played on several
turntables, several prepared-piano pieces and the finale from the 1936
trio. The evening, as described admiringly by Virgil Thomson,
employed 'a large group of players using flowerpots, brake bands,
electric buzzers, drums and similar objects not primarily musical but
capable of producing a wide variety of interesting sounds all the
same'. As critic on the *Herald-Tribune*, after the *Times* the most
influential of New York's daily journals, Thomson became a potent
force for years in promoting Cage's music. 'His work represents …
not only the most advanced methods now in use anywhere but
original expression of the highest poetic quality', wrote Thomson
after a 1945 concert in which a New York audience was first confronted with the sounds of the 'prepared' piano. (A quarter-century
later, however, Thomson was to undergo a change of heart towards
Cage's music. Offended by Cage's later explorations into the use of
electronic devices, he described him as 'a destructive force in music …
a one-way tunnel leading only to the gadget fair'.)

The association with Merce Cunningham, while artistically
productive, also presented Cage with the matter of sexual identity.
Xenia had been a valued partner, and a participant in many of
the percussion concerts. By 1945, however, the relationship with
Cunningham had proven as beneficial personally as artistically; the
time was at hand for a break-up of Cage's marriage. Xenia remained
in New York and became a museum curator; John and Merce took
new quarters on New York's East Side. In that year, too, Cage was to
meet another figure of great influence on his outlooks, the eminent
philosopher Daisetz T. Suzuki, who lectured on Zen Buddhism at

Columbia University. Suzuki's avowed mission was to spread the
teachings of the Zen masters throughout the world in terms that the
layman could understand; his lectures at Columbia were open to all.
'The taste of Zen for me', wrote Cage in his Autobiographical Note,
'comes from the admixture of humour, intransigence and detach-
ment. I have never practised sitting cross-legged, nor do I meditate.
My work is what I do ...' Of Suzuki's teaching he noted that often
'I couldn't for the life of me figure out what he was saying. It was
a week or so later, while I was walking in the woods looking for
mushrooms, that it all dawned on me.'

That work continued to expand, as Cage made his way further
into the outermost realms of creative thought. The year 1948 found
him at another academic hotbed of advanced ideas, comparable to
Cornish in Seattle. At Black Mountain College in North Carolina
Cage taught summer classes for several years, on a faculty that also
included such other progressive notables as the architect Buckminster
Fuller and the visual artists Richard Lippold, Willem de Kooning and
Joseph Albers. There Cage also organized a festival devoted to the
open-textured, quiet, simplistic music of the eccentric French Dada-
inspired composer Erik Satie – half-hour after-dinner concerts
prefaced by Cage's introductory remarks. Satie's music, with its long
stretches of static sound that almost seemed a kind of décor, had
always held a fascination for Cage. 'In the centre of the festival', he
wrote, 'I placed a lecture that opposed Satie and Beethoven and
found that Satie, not Beethoven, was right'.

The fearless pianist David Tudor proved a valuable new addition
to the Cage circle. By 1950 the coterie also included the young
composers Morton Feldman and Christian Wolff, joined soon after
by Earle Brown. They made for a heterogeneous group: Feldman,
with a New York brashness that concealed the quasi-silent musical
miniatures; Wolff, the serious, elegant Frenchman whom Cage once
dubbed 'the most important composer of his generation'; the ascetic
Brown, fascinated at the time by the relationship between Abstract
Expressionism in painting and Schoenbergian atonality; the scholarly,
brilliant pianist Tudor, receptive to the entire gamut of creativity.

They met frequently, in coffee-houses or at one another's
apartments, argued ferociously the merits of each other's latest work
and of music from the outside world as well. They discussed and

Massachusetts born Earle
Brown, *right* (photographed
in 1981), was long one of
Cage's closest associates
calling especially on Cage's
philosophy on the role of
chance and freedom in
determining the course of a
work, as this 'score' of his
December 1952 shows.

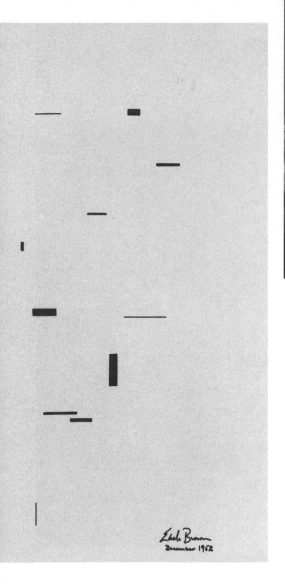

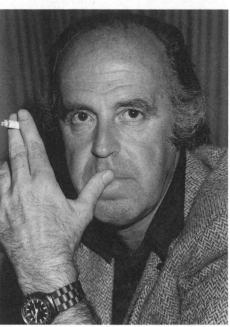

Pianist David Tudor (left)
has been one of Cage's
best-known interpreters.
Here he and Cage
investigate sonorities at a
Japanese temple.

formulated the possibilities of vastly expanding the expressive spectrum by freeing music from such restricting elements as the need
for sounds to relate to one another and thus suggest a perception of
overall structure in the hearer's memory. Magnetic tape had come
along; Edgard Varèse engaged their interest with his electronic studies.
The stronger kinship seemed to exist between Cage's group and
the Abstract Expressionist painters than with most other composers
(Cowell and, sporadically, Varèse excepted). Charles Ives, by 1950
doddering and difficult to approach, showed no interest in the new
generation of musical rebels; if he noticed that some of Cage's
methods had been anticipated in some of his own more adventurous
scores half a century earlier – the leaving of some performance
decisions to the whim of the player, or the admission of silence as a
legitimate component of the musical language – he made no issue of
the matter. In 1950 Cage appeared before Robert Motherwell's Artists'
Club, in what he called *A Lecture on Nothing*. 'I have the feeling
that we are getting nowhere', said John Cage, 'and that is a pleasure'.

Sometime in 1951 Christian Wolff, teaching at Dartmouth College,
introduced Cage to *I Ching*, or *Book of Changes*, the ancient Chinese
oracle, which had just been published in English. No fortune-teller
merely capable of giving yes-and-no answers to simple questions, *I
Ching* communicates through indirection and purposive obfuscation,
leading the questioner to seek out inner resources for dealing with
specific problems: for example, 'Grace has success./In small matters/It
is favourable to undertake something'.) Discovering the book, with its
elaborate system of charts and diagrams, was fortuitously timed; Cage
had been trying out a similar charting system for a set of dances for
Cunningham. Before the year was out he had composed *Music of
Changes*, based on his readings of *I Ching*. The oracle came to
serve Cage as an essential tool, for his music and also for his texts
and artworks.

With or without the oracle, chance operations became a central
element in Cage's music. The year 1951 also saw the creation of the
fourth, and most famous, in a series of *Imaginary Landscapes*, which
he had begun with the help of the radio engineers at the Cornish
School. *Imaginary Landscape No. 4*, introduced to an enthusiastic
crowd (both for and against) at a theatre on the Columbia campus,
is scored for twelve radios, played by twenty-four 'performers'. The

score indicates the exact tuning and volume settings for each performer, but with no foreknowledge of what might be broadcast at
any specific time or place, or whether a station even exists at the given
dial setting. It does, indeed, suggest a landscape: an urban scene,
perhaps an apartment-house courtyard with all windows open and
radios playing.

In the summer of 1952 Cage returned to Black Mountain, where he
accomplished one of the most significant events of his career to date.
In what he later identified as the first 'happening' (although the term
is usually credited to the performance artist Allan Kaprow) Cage
seated the audience 'in four isometric triangular sections, the apexes
of which touched a small square performance area … Disparate activities, dancing by Merce Cunningham, the exhibition of paintings and
the playing of a Victrola by Robert Rauschenberg, Charles Olsen
reading his poetry, or M. C. Richards, atop a ladder, reading hers …
the piano playing of David Tudor, my own reading of a lecture that
included silences … all took place within chance-determined periods
of time'. It was the first attempt at a kind of free-form presentation,
with major decisions only determined at the time of performance by
casting the *I Ching*, that bore the seeds of many of his future works,
even including the *Rolywholyover* circus previously described.

At Black Mountain that summer, Rauschenberg showed Cage his
series of all-black and all-white paintings, which Cage, ever eager for
new pathways, took as yet another source of inspiration. Years before,
in a 1948 essay called *A Composer's Confessions*, he had fantasized about
creating a work of uninterrupted silence, lasting about four minutes
and titled *Silent Prayer*, which he would try to sell to Muzak to serve
as a brief surcease within its endless dribble of building-lobby and
shopping-mall music. Four years later, but with no help from the
background-music industry, he created what came to be his most
famous composition, not merely a measured uninterrupted silence
but a work of four minutes and thirty-three seconds' duration with
the breaks between movements, and even the page-turns, meticulously plotted, deriving its persona from the ambient sounds in the
time and place of performance.

By the time of *4 '33"*, the forty-year-old Cage had amassed enough
fame and/or notoriety to serve any composer in a lifetime. He had
composed nearly 100 pieces, most of them already published by the

Opposite, painter Jasper
Johns has long been another
of Cage's kindred spirits.
This is his *Target with Four
Faces*, 1955, at New York's
Museum of Modern Art.

Cage at work, on his
Sonatas and Interludes,
in 1947

distinguished firm of C. F. Peters. His music for prepared piano alone,
most of it in the form of short études and character-pieces, totalled
several hours' worth; the pianist Maro Ajemian had performed and
recorded one whole set of these works, the *Sonatas and Interludes,* at
New York's Carnegie Hall. Cage had furnished Merce Cunningham's
dancers with a copious repertory, and had composed one orchestral
work of considerable extent, *The Seasons,* for the prestigious New
York group the Ballet Society. He had also earned considerable fame
for his essays and lectures, brilliant in content if sometimes quirky in

form, in which he stated with some eloquence his own singular views on the nature of music.

Those views were, by 1952, well focused on the pathways he had chosen for himself. 'I was to move', he remembered, 'from structure to process, from music as an object having parts to music without beginning, middle or end, music as weather'. He composed the silent piece as meticulously as he had come to work on all his creation, with *I Ching* at his side to assist in major decisions regarding the duration of the separate stretches of silence which formed its several 'movements'.

Random? Haphazard? This page from Cage's *Water Music* shows how carefully he worked out the music on an exact second-by-second time frame.

2. 195

SLAM KEYBOARD LID SHUT (*mf*). (PEDAL)
SHUFFLE DECK OF CARDS; DEAL ⌐⌐ *mp*
INTO PIANO STRINGS: (ALL THIS
AS RAPIDLY AS POSSIBLE)

5.4525   5.5025   5.5525 5.5625

POUR WATER FROM ONE RECEPTACLE TO ANOTHER

POUR WATER

6.215   6.3025   6.40
SIREN-WHISTLE   TURN RADIO OFF

The première of *4 '33 "* was programmed as the final work in a
Cage concert in Woodstock, the upstate New York artists' colony that
would, seventeen years later, give its name to what we might consider
the *Rolywholyover* of rock 'n' roll. The audience was taken aback.
It was accustomed to shock at Cage events, but of a more aggressive
kind; many took the new work as an insult to their expectations.
'Good people of Woodstock', an artist in the audience stood and
exclaimed, 'let's drive these people out of town'.

Over time, however, the work has assumed its rightful importance,
not only in the Cage canon but, more to the point, as a challenge
to anyone's definition of the nature of a musical experience. The
concept of chance, of music arising as an accident beyond the exact
control of the composer, of the conditions for a specific work determined through the casting of the *I Ching*, came increasingly to the
fore in Cage's methodology. So, with ever-increasing force, did the
notion that the substance of a musical work could be whatever the
composer claimed for it: a symphony orchestra playing Mozart, a
four-minute silence, and such in-between events as a man running
a food processor on a stage or telling a story, or the sound of traffic at
a predetermined New York City intersection. The unpredictable
ambient sound at a given time and place, the unpredictable content
of a radio broadcast, the un-predetermined number of performers
present for a particular event (and, in one work, the imperfections on
a piece of cheap manuscript paper that could be read as notes) – all
these chance elements took their place in Cage's definition of his art.
The piece for twelve radios was soon joined by others: in 1955, *Speech*
for five radios and a news-reader; in 1958, *Music Walk* for one or
more pianists at a single piano, with radios and phonographs; in
1960, *Cartridge Music*, employing small objects inserted into an old-
fashioned phonograph cartridge, for any number of players and
loudspeakers. Several works – *Atlas Eclipticalis* for orchestra and the
nearly three hours of the *Études Australes* for piano – were created
from pages chosen by *I Ching* from star atlases, with the maps transferred to transparent paper and superimposed over music paper so
that the celestial dots could be read as notes.

In his enormously influential collection of essays called *Silence*,
published in 1961 but containing material – from lectures at Cornish,
concert programmes on both coasts and articles in avant-garde

publications – dating from as far back as 1937, Cage defined his intention '… to affirm this life, not to bring order out of chaos … but simply to wake up to the very life we're living, which is so excellent once one lets it … act of its own accord'. Whatever difficulties the music of Cage may present to the innocent listener, the material of *Silence* captivates immediately with its wisdom, its childlike desire to see all, to find a macrocosm of delight in a microcosm of imagery. 'Where do we go from here?' Cage constantly asks. 'Towards theatre', is one reply; that art more than music resembles nature. We have eyes as well as ears, and it is our business while we are alive to use them'.

The transition 'from structure to process' was dramatized – even theatricalized – throughout the 1950s and beyond, by an astounding succession of works, most of them bearing 'generic' titles referring to their duration: *59 1/2 for a String Player, 34′ 46.776″ for prepared piano*, etc. They may not leap into brimming life from their verbal description but at least clearly suggest the lively, if madcap, obsessions of their inventor. In its existence as abstract, or generically titled creation – Music for Piano, Solo for Voice, Variation III, 'any number of people performing any actions' – much of Cage's output at this time did, indeed, seem to 'act of its own accord'. The intent was to allow an audience to invent its role as participant in the music-making process, free from the preconceptions a programmatic title might suggest, and to offer music as a two-sided mirror, reflecting the giver as much as the recipient. The process implied a measure of listener co-operation that could not automatically be expected from a 1960s audience spoiled by easy access to recognized masterpieces through radio broadcasts, recordings and the growing impact of television. Cage's musical escapades were constantly beset by the possible perception that he might, indeed, be merely a madman, or at least a charlatan.

His own ever-widening circle offered support and protection. New York in the 1960s relished newness. Conformity and conservatism, emanating from the political doldrums of the preceding decade, gave way to a passion for trends, which sometimes seemed to engender a new one every week: Pop art, Op art, totally serialized music, musical anarchy, mixed-media, happenings, the rediscovery of medieval music. Much of Cage's success stemmed from his eloquence in stating his case: the charm of his essays and lectures with their soft-spoken

Following page, Cage's Variations is a series of unconnected works, each demanding a special time and place. Variations I dates from 1958.

JOHN CAGE

\# In preparation
= 2 copies needed for performance
+ Available for rental
* Facsimile photostat copies, including any plastic transparencies
   necessary for performance
   Prices are available upon request

PIANO AND HARPSICHORD
(see also: PREPARED PIANO)

I. Solo

*4'33" (1952) (tacet, any instrument or combination of instruments)
   (Peters 6777)
*4'33" (No. 2) (1962) (0'00") (Peters 6796)
   Solo to be performed in any way by anyone
*CHEAP IMITATION (1969) (Peters 6605)
*DREAM (1948) (5 min) (Peters 6707)
*ELECTRONIC MUSIC FOR PIANO (1965) (Peters 6801)
*FOR M. C. AND D. T. (1952) (2 min) (Peters 6713)
*FOR PAUL TAYLOR AND ANITA DENCKS (1957) (3 min) (Peters 6715)
*IN A LANDSCAPE (1948) (8 min) (Peters 6725)
*METAMORPHOSIS (1938) (15 min) (Peters 6723)
*MUSIC FOR PIANO 1 (1952) (4 min) (Peters 6729)
*MUSIC FOR PIANO 2 (1953) (4 min) (Peters 6730)
*MUSIC FOR PIANO 3 (1953) (Peters 6731)
*MUSIC FOR PIANO 20 (1953) (Peters 6733)
   MUSIC OF CHANGES (1951) (43 min). 4 Volumes (Peters 6256, 6257,
   6258, 6259)
\#OPHELIA (1946) (5 min) (Peters 6788)
*A ROOM (1943) (2 min) (Peters 6790)
*THE SEASONS, Ballet in One Act (1947) (15 min) (Peters 6744)
   (see also: Orchestra)
*SEVEN HAIKU (1952) (3 min) (Peters 6745)
   SOLO FOR PIANO (1957-58) (Peters 6705) (see also: Orchestra)
*SUITE FOR TOY PIANO (or Piano) (1948) (8 min) (Peters 6258)
*TV KÖLN (1958) (Peters 6764)
*WAITING (1952) (1 min) (Peters 6769)
*WATER MUSIC (1952) (Peters 6770) (see: Audio-Visual)

II. Solo or Ensemble

* EXPERIENCES I (1945-48) (6 min) (Peters 6766a)
   Duo for 2 pianos
*HPSCHD (1967-69) (Peters 6804)
   7 harpsichord soloists and 51 tapes
*MUSIC FOR PIANO 4-19 (1953) (Peters 6712)
*MUSIC FOR PIANO 21-36; 37-52 (1955) (Peters 6734)
*MUSIC FOR PIANO 53-68 (1956) (Peters 6735)
*MUSIC FOR PIANO 69-84 (1956) (Peters 6736)
   to be performed, in whole or part, by any number of pianists
*MUSIC WALK (1958) (Peters 6739) (see: Audio-Visual)
*VARIATIONS I (1958); VARIATIONS II (1961) (Peters 6767, 6268)
   (see: Instrumental Solo and Chamber Music; Various Ensembles)
*WINTER MUSIC (1957) (Peters 6775) (see also: Orchestra)
   to be performed, in whole or part, by 1 to 20 pianists

PREPARED PIANO
(see also: ORCHESTRA
[Concerto for Prepared Piano and Chamber Orchestra])

I. Solo

*31'57.9864" (1954) (see: Instrumental Solo and Chamber Music;
   Various Ensembles) (Peters 6780)
*34'46.776" (1954) (see: Instrumental Solo and Chamber Music;
   Various Ensembles) (Peters 6781)
   AMORES (1943) (9 min) (Peters 6264)
   2 Solos for prepared piano, with the addition of
   2 Trios for percussion

*BACCHANALE (1938) (6 min) (Peters 6748)
*DAUGHTERS OF THE LONESOME ISLE (1945) (5 min) (Peters 6785)
*MEDITATION (1943) (1 min) (Peters 6787)
*MUSIC FOR MARCEL DUCHAMP (1947) (5 min) (Peters 6767)
*THE PERILOUS NIGHT (1944) (15 min) (Peters 6757)
*PRELUDE FOR MEDITATION (1944) (1 min) (Peters 6786)
*ROOT OF AN UNFOCUS (1944) (4 min) (Peters 6760)
*TOTEM ANCESTOR (1942) (2 min) (Peters 6762)
*TRIPLE-PACED (1944) (1 min) (Peters 6763)
*VALENTINE OUT OF SEASON (1944) (3 min) (Peters 6765)

II. Duo for 2 Pianos, 4 Hands

*A BOOK OF MUSIC (1944) (20 min) (Peters 6749)
*THREE DANCES (1945) (20 min) (Peters 6750)

PERCUSSION

(see also: Orchestra, Chamber Music, Theatrical Ensembles)

*AMORES (1943) (9 min) (Peters 6264)
*CREDO IN US (1942) (4 min) (Peters 6265)
*DOUBLE MUSIC (with Lou Harrison) (1941)
   made by 4 percussionists (Peters 6758)
*FIRST CONSTRUCTION (IN METAL) (1939) (Peters 6752)
*IMAGINARY LANDSCAPE No. 1 (1939) (6 min) (Peters 6716)
   (see also: Audio-Visual)
*SHE IS ASLEEP (1943) (Peters 6759)
   I. Quartet (12 tom-toms) (8 min)
   II. Duet (voice and prepared piano)
*SOLO FOR VOICE 1 (1958) (Peters 6750)
   to be performed alone or with any part of CONCERT
*SOLO FOR VOICE 2 (1960) (Peters 6751)
   GAMELAN MUSIC
*THE WONDERFUL WIDOW OF EIGHTEEN SPRINGS (1942) (3 min)
   (closed piano) (2 min) (words by James Joyce) (Peters 6270)
*SONG BOOKS (1970) (2 volumes) (Peters 6806)
*THIRTY-TWO MELODIES FOR VOICE AND PIANO (1938)
   (Peters 6806)

INSTRUMENTAL SOLO AND CHAMBER MUSIC
(see also: Orchestra, Various Ensembles)

*ATLAS ECLIPTICALIS (Concert for Piano and Orchestra)

Strings

*59½" (1953) (see: Various Ensembles) (Peters 6775)
*26'1.1499" (1955) (see: Various Ensembles) (Peters 6775)
*NOCTURNE FOR VIOLIN AND PIANO (1947) (Various) (Peters 6745)
*SIX MELODIES FOR VIOLIN AND KEYBOARD PIANO (1950)
   (15 min) (Peters 6744)
*STRING QUARTET IN FOUR PARTS (1950) (20 min) (Peters 6752)

Winds

*MUSIC FOR WIND INSTRUMENTS (1937) (8 min)
   (Peters 6738b Score; Peters 6738 Parts)
   I. Trio (Fl, Cl in B♭, Bsn)
   II. Duo (Ob, Hrn)
   III. Quintet (Fl, Ob, Cl in B♭, Hrn, Bsn)
*SONATA FOR CLARINET (Solo) (1933) (6 min) (Peters 6753)
*THREE PIECES FOR FLUTE DUET (1935) (6 min) (Peters 6761)

VARIATIONS I,

FOR DAVID TUDOR

SIX SQUARES OF TRANSPARENT MATERIAL, ONE HAVING POINTS
OF 4 SIZES: THE 13 VERY SMALL ONES ARE SINGLE SOUNDS; THE
7 SMALL BUT LARGER ONES ARE 2 SOUNDS; THE 3 OF GREATER
SIZE ARE 3 SOUNDS; THE 4 LARGEST 4 OR MORE SOUNDS. PLUR-
ALITIES ARE PLAYED TOGETHER OR AS "CONSTELLATIONS." IN
USING PLURALITIES, AN EQUAL NUMBER OF THE 5 OTHER SQUARES
(HAVING 5 LINES EACH) ARE TO BE USED FOR DETERMINATIONS,
OR EQUAL NUMBER OF POSITIONS, - EACH SQUARE HAVING 4.
THE 5 LINES ARE: LOWEST FREQUENCY, SIMPLEST OVERTONE
STRUCTURE, GREATEST AMPLITUDE, LEAST DURATION, AND
EARLIEST OCCURENCE WITHIN A DECIDED UPON TIME.
PERPENDICULARS FROM POINTS TO LINES GIVE DISTANCES
TO BE MEASURED OR SIMPLY OBSERVED. ANY NUMBER OF
PERFORMERS; ANY KIND AND NUMBER OF INSTUMENTS.

ON HIS BIRTHDAY (TARDILY), JANUARY 1958

John Cage

2-
3-
4-
5-
-

assertions that the aim of all music should be to bridge the gap between art and life. Such statements also went some distance to bridge the gap between Cage and the outside world, as he presented that world with, for example, the work called *o′oo″* in which he appeared on-stage feeding vegetables into an electric blender, feeding the whirring of the machinery into loudspeakers and, of course, drinking the juice; or another work called, understandably, *Indeterminacy*, consisting of ninety anecdotes, each lasting exactly a minute, spoken by Cage while David Tudor's piano meandered through deliberating non-matching music as if on another planet. 'Everything we do is music' became, of all Cage's quotations, the one most often trumpeted.

The coming of tape broadened even further the range of what Cage might include under the rubric of music. In 1958 he accepted the invitation of Luciano Berio, one of Italy's musical radicals, to investigate the potential of working with tape at the new electronic studio maintained by Radio Milan. (While in Milan, too, Cage became a celebrity in another congenial field, employing his expertise in wild mushroom recognition, and his adequate command of Italian, to win the top prize in a popular television quiz show. During his weeks as a contestant he also got to demonstrate a prepared piano and to create a multimedia piece involving cooking utensils, a goose-whistle and a bathtub.)

As early as 1951 Cage had experimented with the juxtaposition of tape tracks, creating in his *Williams Mix* a dense collage of overlay determined by mathematical permutations. Seven years later, tape technology had outstripped the devices in *Williams Mix*. At the Milan studio Cage created his *Fontana Mix* (named after the owner of his *pensione*), which was to become the model for several of his later collage works; the term 'mix' itself became anchored in Cage's musical vocabulary from this time on. The music was sketched out on a series of transparencies, which could be placed on top of one another in any number of ways. Each of the possible 'readings' then became the basis for a tape, with the sounds themselves produced either by electronic means or by a recording of natural objects (similar to the *musique concrète* methods Edgard Varèse had used in the electronic sections of his *Déserts*).

Speaking (in admiration) at a Cage concert soon after the Milan adventures, Henry Cowell made the comment that the value in Cage's

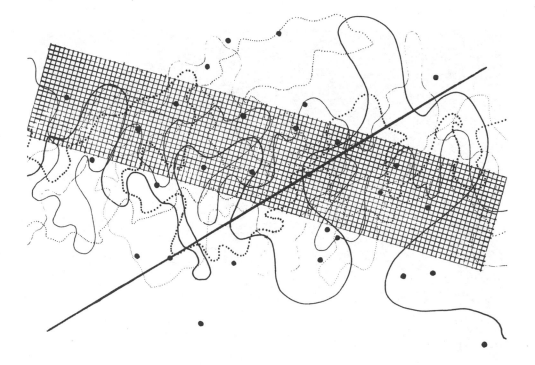

Fontana Mix calls for a four-track tape, whose recorded material is determined by overlaying a series of transparencies (see p. 139 for a different configuration of them). The title came from the hotel at which Cage stayed in Milan while developing the 'mix' at the Italian Radio station.

music, and that of his close associates Morton Feldman, Earle Brown and Christian Wolff was that they had 'gotten rid of the glue'. The fate of *Fontana Mix* and its concomitant works nicely underscores Cowell's observation, and also Cage's expressed concern that prized process over structure. 'Where people had felt the necessity to stick sounds together to make a continuity', Cage wrote in answer to Cowell's comment, 'we four felt the opposite necessity to get rid of the glue so that sounds would be themselves'.

In its 'pure' form the *Fontana Mix* consists of a four-track tape, derived from superimposed transparencies out of sound sources at hand; in a recording from the early 1960s (on the Time label, no longer available) the 'mix' is taken mostly from fragments of radio broadcasts. In that performance the resultant tape is combined with another Cage work, the *Aria* composed at about the same time ('for singer of any register, to any text'), performed on the recording by the remarkable Cathy Berberian (formerly the wife of Luciano Berio) with her own free-associative text, a hilarious conflation of bits and pieces of selected clichés from radio soap-operas, magazine

Of the many dance pieces
produced by John Cage
and Merce Cunningham in
tandem, *Walkaround Time*
may be the most complex
and the most popular. It was
created in 1968.

By 1966 the world had caught up with Cage; electronic music, chance music, 'happenings', all of which he had explored years ago, were now in vogue.

advertisements and the like: a collage atop a collage. The *Aria*, furthermore, could also be woven into yet another Cage work, the *Concert* for piano; that work, in turn, could also be performed as a solo, or with orchestral instruments.

The basis of Cage's own anarchy became, furthermore, the cause of all anarchies. His fascination with Satie's music, above all its ability to stir the spirit with the barest minimum of sound and artfully shaped silence, continued unabated. In 1963 Cage lured several of his friends to a modest theatre on New York's Lower Eastside, to present, over a twenty-four-hour uninterrupted stretch, the most notorious of Satie's works, a page-long piano piece called *Vexations*, whose instructions stipulated that it be performed 840 times. It was a sublime addition to the annals of the 'happenings' that were stirring the New York soul at the time.

The kind of musical anarchism embodied in these works fitted the craving for adventure rampant in the American avant garde throughout the 1960s. *HPSCHD*, which Cage created with the electronic pioneer Lejaren Hiller in his studio at the University of Illinois, went an even greater distance to appease that craving: it was a monster complex of sight and sound. Seven harpsichordists played chance-

selected music by Mozart, Bach, Schoenberg and others; fifty-one
tapes resonated through as many loudspeakers; films, slides and
coloured lights filled the performance area; relationship between
events was fluid, indeterminate, chance-based. Reviewing the event
for the *New York Times*, Richard Kostelanetz wrote of 'an atonal
and structural chaos ... continually in flux', and found the sound
'rather mellow, except for blasts of ear-piercing feedback'.

In 1967 the poet Wendell Berry presented Cage with a copy of *The
Journals of Henry David Thoreau*, who more than a century before
had asserted his rights as an individualist, free to pursue a life in a
forest cabin, to study and write about nature and to protest against
his country's involvement in foreign entanglements he considered
improper. As with all his 'discoveries' – percussion, the prepared
piano, tape – Cage immediately immersed himself feverishly in
Thoreau; the anarchistic spirit that motivated the nineteenth-century
free-thinker seemed to Cage the exact mirror of his own. In 1970, in
a huge collection called, simply *Song Books* ('solos for voice 3–92, to
be sung with or without other indeterminate music, in any order, by
one or more singers') Cage took key phrases from Thoreau – most
of all his *Essay on Civil Disobedience* – fragmented them, thinned
the texture down at times as an implied tribute to fellow anarchist
Erik Satie, and produced a tribute to free thought in its many manifestations. Another work from four years later, *Empty Words*, offered
an even more inscrutable mixture: a non-syntactical pot-pourri using
single letters, syllables and words from Thoreau, to be performed
by itself or stirred into a mixture of moments from the *Song Books* (as
they are on a Wergo recording, with the *Empty Words* read by Cage
himself). From Thoreau's writing, too, Cage unearthed another
valuable quotation to annex to his own philosophy. 'Music is
continuous', wrote the great New England rebel. 'Only listening
is intermittent.'

The USA celebrated its Bicentennial in 1976. Despite his presence
on the edge of musical chaos, Cage had become a name to reckon
with among American composers, and he received two major com-
missions to honour the event. One resulted in the most all-embracing
of the Thoreau-inspired works; Cage called it, simply, *Lecture on
Weather*. Commissioned by the Canadian Broadcasting System, the
Lecture combined twelve collages of text fragments from Thoreau

with an abstract nature film by Luis Frangella and an imaginative tape
recording of rain, thunder and other meteorological phenomena.
The other work took Cage into the world of the symphony orchestra,
which he had previously explored to only a limited extent.

Cage's music was still, and was fated to remain, *terra incognita* to
symphony audiences whose greatest pleasure came from rehearing
familiar and established masterworks. One famous instance, the New
York première in 1964 of *Atlas Eclipticalis*, led by Leonard Bernstein,
might have frightened off the staunchest explorer, with over half the
audience exiting during the work and the rest remaining to boo
loudly at the end. 'If Mr. Cage had attached bells to the exit doors',
one critic noted, 'they would have drowned out the music'.

Nevertheless, twelve years later a consortium of six American
orchestras commissioned a major orchestral work from Cage; this
actually produced two works in one, playable – in true Cage fashion –
singly, successively or simultaneously. *Renga*, the first, used as its
inspiration a collection of Thoreau drawings, whose outlines became
melodic shapes; *Apartment House, 1776* wove a panorama of folk-
songs, live or recorded, into an orchestral texture. It also proved to be
a disaster; few members of symphony concert audiences in the USA
knew more about Cage than that he was a fearsome innovator at the
extreme edge of the avant garde. The performance by the Los Angeles
Philharmonic, which had never before touched a note of Cage or his
cohorts, again provoked not so much a riot as a mass exodus, and
the scene was re-enacted in other halls during the work's brief career.

If *Renga* was to make no headway in concert halls, at least the
exquisite calligraphy of the score stirred admiration in an exhibition
of Cage manuscripts, in 1977, at the Museum of Modern Art – where
Cage had had his first New York concert thirty-four years earlier. In
1977, too, he began work on a set of 'Freeman' Études for solo violin.
Unlike his 'free-choice' works the études were designed to be played as
written, if possible; Cage thus reverted to a traditional manuscript
style, writing out the notes in the traditional, determinate notation
that he had virtually abandoned in favour of more graphic styles.
Commissioned by the Los Angeles patron and photographer Betty
Freeman, the 'Freeman' Études stand as very likely the most
demanding works ever composed for violin or, more than likely, for
any instrument. 'I wanted to make the music as difficult as possible',

said Cage, 'so that a performance would show that the impossible is not impossible, and to write thirty-two of them'. As if to balance the restrictions posed by these works, Cage worked simultaneously on an exactly opposite kind of music, in which contingency and result can be widely separated. One result was *Inlets*, a piece for conch shells filled with water, which can be tipped to allow for gurgles.

Yet another phenomenon came into Cage's life around this time the ever-more-sophisticated technology of the computer, capable of coping with his voracious appetite for acquiring and then manipulating information. Cage had met Pierre Boulez years before; while the two men stood at opposing points as regard strictness versus freedom in musical structure, they recognized each other's importance. Boulez had established in Paris the 'Institute for Computer Research in Acoustics and Music' (IRCAM); it quickly became a leader in the worldwide quest to redefine the very nature of music while expanding its expressive boundaries. Cage, of course, had been doing the same, largely without electronic assistance, for most of his life.

Yet he, too, saw new horizons revealed by this wondrous technology. One associate had created a computer program for casting *I Ching*, closely approximating the randomizing capabilities of the traditional methods of casting. Cage had also enlisted the computer's help in finishing the set of 'Freeman' Études; the music, he admitted, had almost outstripped his own understanding of what these dense, convoluted pieces were all about. Now, at IRCAM, he set about creating another of his huge panoramas, using words and music in a constantly shifting relationship, defying rational analysis as to its proper classification. *Roaratorio*, an Irish Circus on *Finnegans Wake* as the new work was called, drew upon Joyce's enigmatic masterpiece that had long been in Cage's own pantheon of companionable influences. Its substance was the book itself: several thousand sounds mentioned in the text or recorded in places referred to by Joyce: a joyous, romping roar of an oratorio, pieced together with the invaluable assistance of Boulez's computers. To compile this gigantic collage, Cage contacted radio stations or performing groups in every place, however small, mentioned in the book; from around the world, the sounds of folk-singers, brass bands, pub crowds, pipers, fiddles and you-name-it poured into Cage's studio space at IRCAM. As it was assembled, with decisions as to what-goes-where shared by Cage and IRCAM's computers, Cage himself read the narration of Joyce's own words, affecting an Irish brogue with some success. After the work had been performed, to enormous acclaim, Cage set about drawing up a publishable score, to serve not only as a guide for setting James Joyce to music, but as a way of creating a comparable piece of work from any book, through computer technology.

Against the continued stiff resistance of the musical 'establishment', Cage's fame continued to grow. Some of his early admirers, certainly, became somewhat more cautious in the light of later experiments. Virgil Thomson's famous article of 'recantation', *Cage and the Collage of Noises*, first appeared in 1970, and caused a bitter rift between the former friends that was never completely healed. Thomson wrote:

He thinks of himself as music's corrective, as a prophet denouncing the whole of Renaissance and post-Renaissance Europe, with its incorrigible respect for beauty and distinction, and dissolving all that in an ocean of electronic availabilities ... It is not the first time that an artist has fancied himself as destroying the past, and then found himself using it ... Destroying the past is a losing game. The past cannot be destroyed; it merely wears out ... He is also a major musical force and a leader among us'

For every renegade there seemed to be a hundred recruits; in March 1982, to initiate Cage's seventieth birthday celebrations, a converted New York cinema palace called Symphony Space held a 'Wall-to-Wall Cage' concert, twenty-four hours in which crowds waited continuously outdoors in the cold, hoping (mostly in vain) for a relinquished seat. Another concert a few weeks later, this time lasting a mere ten hours, drew similar crowds.

Was there any territory in the arts that Cage had, by his seventieth birthday, left unexplored? He had, after all, dabbled in painting since his early years; his written works added up to a considerable volume of literature. He had manifested certain prowess in the culinary arts. He himself had propounded the belief in theatre as the most sovereign of all the arts. Yet, there was one realm left to explore: opera. Cage had never expressed a fondness for the form, discerning in opera

Critic Virgil Thomson (right) was not one of Cage's most ardent admirers, yet in 1990 Cage could still flash his famous grin in Thomson's presence.

'everything that's wrong with European music'; yet, by the mid-1980s he had hit upon a way to deal with the medium, and perhaps even to delight a few anti-operatic souls like himself. Armed with *I Ching* as an aide in making choices, Cage took on the realm of existing European opera, confining himself to works old enough to be free of copyright, amassing a collection of famous and not-so-famous arias which he then distributed to cast and orchestra. As with the Thoreau and Joyce pieces, the *Europeras* were a series of collages, in which familiar music was heard in unfamiliar ways – a baritone taking on an aria meant for soprano, perhaps, with an orchestral accompaniment from an entirely different aria – and with no connection between any chosen aria and the assumed dramatic situation (for which Cage had dreamed up his own hilarious pastiche plots by combining single sentences from pre-existing operatic scenarios). The musical content could vary from day to day, with *I Ching* enlisted before each performance to decide what music would be performed and in what order. The first two *Europeras*, staged in Frankfurt in 1987 (by a narrow escape after the intended house was torched by an arsonist) employed large casts and elaborate scenery, with the orchestra broken into groups and scattered around the stage. *Europeras* Nos. 3 and 4, first produced at London's Almeida Festival in 1990, used smaller casts, no scenery, and with some of the music emanating from old gramophones playing 78-rpm recordings of classic aria performances. None

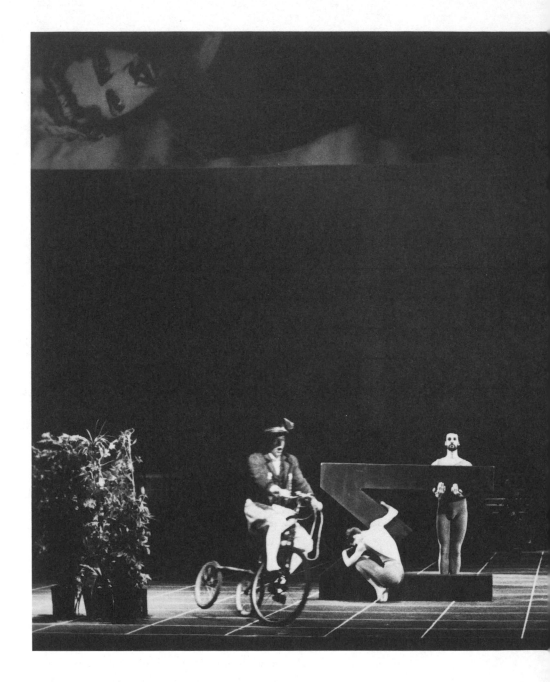

Cage's five *Europeras* were elaborate collage pieces involving snippets from dozens of pre-existing operas bundled together in appealing and original ways. The first two, first heard in Frankfurt in 1987, came to America the following year in one of the great Pepsico Summerfare Festivals.

of the works, therefore, conveyed any sort of narrative in the customary operatic sense; what made them work was the constant interplay of musical textures, and of the familiar and unfamiliar, the moments when, after a thick overlay of half-a-dozen arias sung at once, a single line of music – a Mozart aria, or a phrase from Saint-Saëns' *Samson et Dalila* – hung suspended in silence.

In 1988 Cage was invited to deliver the Norton Lectures at Harvard, a distinction formerly enjoyed by Igor Stravinsky and Leonard Bernstein. Typically, of course, Cage devised his own manner of delivery. The series bore the title:

MethodStructureIntentionDisciplineNotationIndeterminacyInterpenet rationImitationDevotionCircumstancesVariableStructureNonunderstandi ngContingencyInconsistencyPerformance

Lifetime collaborators Cage (right) and Merce Cunningham, photographed at New York's Lincoln Center in 1978

(with no space between words). Each lecture was devised according to an orthographic trick that Cage had been playing with for years: a layout on the page such that the key words 'method', 'structure', etc.

ran in a vertical column in the centre of each line, as in this from the start of 'structure':

'include it**S**
       Top
to console you**R**self with the
    even **U**nder what
  was quite ne**C**essary …'

Operating from the term 'acrostic' in which the first letter of each line spells out a vertical message, Cage named his creation 'mesostic'. The six Norton Lectures, as published, occupy 420 large pages of mesostic, all built upon the words in the overall title of the lecture and none other.

As his eightieth birthday approached, Cage continued to broaden the scope of his interests and, consequently, of his activities. He began an extensive new series of musical compositions, instrumental works adaptable for performance by any number of players, bearing the generic title 'Music for …' For these works, performable by an indeterminate number of players, Cage provided no notated score, only a set of parts for whatever instruments are at hand, marked off in time segments. Each musician carries a stopwatch; each can decide when to begin and end. 'Each player', Cage further stipulated, 'should prepare his part by himself; there should be no joint rehearsal until all parts have been carefully prepared. They are then to be played as if from six centers in space.'

He revived his old interest in painting, and began a series of watercolours at Mountain Lake, Virginia, in 1988. A year later, in between receiving prizes in the USA and Japan, he collaborated with Merce Cunningham and Jasper Johns on a gala event to 'celebrate Cage'; it was mounted in London and Liverpool. In 1991 there was *Beach Birds*, yet another collaboration with Cunningham, the great constant in Cage's life since their meeting in Seattle fifty-three years earlier. The Zürich Festival devoted its entire run to Cage and Joyce. Meanwhile, Cage had begun work, with the Los Angeles Museum of Contemporary Art, on *Rolywholyover   A Circus*, an exhibition within museum walls that would still, however, capture his creative spirit on the wing. In one sense, he was not present at the opening. In another, he was.

'What can be analyzed in my work, or criticized' Cage wrote in his 1989 Autobiographical Note, 'are the questions that I ask. And that would make the difference between one composition made with chance operations and another. That is, the principle underlying the results of these chance operations is the questions ...' Of all questions asked by Cage, or asked implicitly in his works, the most basic, it seems, is this: 'Why not?'

6

Composer Harry Partch
prided himself no less on his
music than the fanciful
instruments he designed for it.
With conductor Jack Logan,
Partch examines his
'Quadrangularis Reversum',
a large marimba-like instrument made entirely of wood.

*Don't put down the hybrids, because there isn't
anything else*

Lou Harrison in the BBC
documentary *West Coast Story,* 1987

New Sources, New Sounds

In the spring of 1889 the city of Paris produced its Exposition
Universelle. Ostensibly a celebration of the centennial of the French
Revolution, this acre-upon-acre display of world culture also opened
the eyes and ears of its thirty million visitors to the vastness and
variety of life beyond the experience of the Western world. Musicians
and dancers from Asia, Africa and the Pacific regions performed their
own music. Sample landscapes from exotic regions, including an
entire street from Cairo complete with donkey carts and beggars, were
constructed on a field mere kilometres from the up-to-date bustle of
downtown Paris. At one end of the fair the mysteries of ancient
worlds had been recreated for the wonderment of audiences; at the

The 1889 Universal
Exposition brought Parisians
face-to-face with exotic
cultures from around the
world for the first time; the
young Claude Debussy
was one of thousands of
enthralled spectators. This
is the Hawaiian Pavilion.

other end the brand-new Eiffel Tower also basked in the wonderment of its first observers.

The display of non-Western artworks was an array of artistry and artistic outlooks beyond anything in the previous experience of Western observers. The painter Henri Rousseau found a kindred spirit in the primitivism of African paintings and sculptures; so did the sculptor Auguste Rodin. The 27-year-old Claude Debussy was enchanted by the sounds of Chinese and Indonesian music; they were all new to him, as to most composers in the West, but he soon found ways to blend these new discoveries into his own music: piano pieces with Oriental titles (e.g., *Pagodes*) and Oriental-sounding scales and melodies. Other French composers echoed his fascination with the music of other worlds: Charles Koechelin (in a series of pieces to 'illustrate' Rudyard Kipling's *Jungle Book*) and Maurice Ravel.

The Western world had, of course, known something of the art of non-Western lands for several decades preceding the Paris exposition. The opening of Japan to international trade earlier in the century had produced a veritable craze for anything associated with that country. The mania for 'all one sees that's Japanese' even turned up, deliciously parodied, in several of the Gilbert and Sullivan comic operettas. Even so, the 1889 World's Fair marks a moment of significance for the serious amalgamation of non-Western musical ideas and Western music. By the end of the century, inspired by the opportunities revealed by the Exposition Universelle, scholars had taken primitive recording equipment to Asia and Africa, and brought back recordings to astound listeners and inspire composers in Europe and America; these early samplings became the foundation for the new science of ethnomusicology.

Of all the musics to reach out to Western ears from their native milieu, none seemed more attractive, and more likely to inspire Western imitations, than the music of Indonesia, the gamelans of Bali and Java. It is easy to understand why; of all non-Western musical cultures, Indonesia had the most in common with Western ideas: a written-down, highly systematized music, a complex and sophisticated system of orchestration that could even be somewhat imitated by the sounds of Western instruments. There are differences among the musical styles of separate Indonesian regions; the music of Java, for example, differs in subtle respects from the music of Bali.

Following page, a Balinese ensemble playing the trompong, an assemblage of kettle-shaped gongs suspended on a wood frame, tuned over a range of two octaves: Colin McPhee's book Music in Bali describes in great detail the composer's fascinated discovery of the rich sounds of the Indonesian gamelan.

What they share, however, is the gamelan, the performing ensemble capable of myriad varieties of sound, its tradition dating back many centuries.

The gamelan is an orchestra, consisting for the most part of percussion instruments – drums, gongs, xylophones, possibly augmented by wind instruments and singers. It differs from a Western orchestra both in sound – the wonderful percussive jangle – and philosophy. Every gamelan is conceived as a unit; the instruments are fashioned and tuned to go together, and cannot be transferred from one gamelan to another. Their music is built out of systems that can be traced back a millennium or more, so that new compositions are not usually very different from very old ones.

It is not difficult to imagine how this kind of music, hypnotic, exhilarating, intricately patterned (similar to the Indonesian batik fabric designs), could seize the attention of composers half a world away. Edgard Varèse, for a time a Debussy protégé, absorbed the older master's fascination with Asian music and spread his enthusiasms to his new circle of associates after his emigration to the USA. What appealed to Varèse in particular was not merely the exotic, repetitive patterns of Asian music; above all, it was his realization that complex musical systems could exist and foster masterful compositions without connection to the twelve-note scale of Western music and the sophisticated harmonic systems composers had derived from it. In his own music – the fearsome array of percussion in such works as *Amériques* and *Ionisation* and his use of primitive electronic devices like the theremin and the ondes martenot – Varèse had already breached the boundaries of Western harmony and instrumentation; the new imports from Asia and Africa showed him the worlds that lay beyond those boundaries.

The fascination with the newly discovered musics found its firmest stronghold among composers on the American West Coast, a region already inundated with Asian awareness. Henry Cowell's *Ostinato pianissimo* of 1934, a pioneering work in the use of a self-sufficient percussion orchestra, is clearly beholden to sounds of the gamelan. Furthermore, it spawned similar works by the Cowell protégés John Cage and his colleague Lou Harrison who scandalized San Francisco audiences late in the 1930s with their all-percussion concerts, with many of the 'instruments' made over from discarded automobile

parts. Moreover, the 'prepared piano' works that Cage composed early
in his career – with piano strings invaded with various small objects
to alter their pitch and resonance – produced sounds easily mistaken
for those of a gamelan.

Of the numerous Western composers captivated by the potential
offered by Indonesia's gamelans, two can be said to have been most
deeply affected: the Canadian-born Colin McPhee and the West-
Coast American Harrison, born a generation apart but united in their
musical passions. Born in Toronto but active for most of his life in
the USA, McPhee (1900–64) was at first routinely educated along
conservative paths, as composer and piano virtuoso. In New York in
the 1920s he was an active participant in new-music concert organizations, produced two piano concertos and a symphony (all now lost)
and, more important, explored the potential of composing for
unconventional instrumental groups through his studies with the
formidable Edgard Varèse.

In 1931 McPhee heard, for the first time, recordings of Balinese
gamelans, and this discovery became the decisive event in his career.
By year's end he had moved to Bali, where he remained, with a
few brief excursions homeward, for seven years. His book, *A House
in Bali*, enchantingly accounts the experience of an American

Members of the gamelan
named 'gong gedé', a
sacred ensemble at Gianjar,
Bali, photographed by
Colin McPhee in 1935

successfully blending into an exotic civilization. In his years on Bali, McPhee collected and transcribed some of that island's music and, in collaboration with the noted anthropologist Margaret Mead, motivated the natives to renew respect for their musical traditions (which were on the wane). McPhee actually founded several gamelans on Bali, composed his own music in the Balinese style (but for Western instruments) and produced what remains the definitive scholarly study of Balinese music.

In fact, McPhee did not compose very much Bali-inspired music of his own; his pioneering work consisted mostly of studies into the nature of the source material and, after his return to America, of lectures and teaching. His single well-known work, *Tabuh-tabuhan*, stands as a unique landmark of transcultural hybridization: an orchestral tone poem lasting about eighteen minutes, composed in 1936 during a visit to Mexico, though thoroughly permeated with the sense of Balinese place. Alongside the standard symphony orchestra, there is a 'nuclear gamelan' (two pianos, celesta, xylophone, marimba and glockenspiel); this orchestral sub-group serves to imitate the intricate, chime-like figuration of some of the gamelan instruments. The larger orchestra includes two authentic Balinese gongs; the light

Saron (tuned bronze slabs resting on rattan in a wood trough), and the trompong in the gamelan 'luang' at Singapadu Village, Bali, from Colin McPhee's collection

1. and 2. gangsas chenik and kantilans, divided
3. and 4. gangsas gedé and penyachahs, divided
5. jublags
6. jegogans
7. gendèrs barangan
8. gendèrs gedé
9. kelenang
10. kajar
11. kemong
12. kempur
13. kendangs L. and W.; tut-dag interplay
14. rinchik and gentorak

Left, inspired by the beauty and strength of the music he heard in Indonesia, Colin McPhee transcribed some of it into Western notation; this piece is from Kuta Village. *Below,* a musician in the gamelan 'Selundeng' strikes the metal bars of the nyonyong with a wooden mallet.

sounds of Balinese hand-beaten drums translates in McPhee's orchestration to pizzicato cellos and basses, low harp and staccato piano
tones. Much of the work is based on authentic Balinese music that
McPhee had collected and transcribed, its delicate tracery nicely
worked into the context of a Western orchestra. After its Mexican
première (performed, almost before the ink was dry, by Carlos Chávez
and the National Orchestra of Mexico City), *Tabuh-tabuhan* made its
way slowly. Its first United States performance was not until 1953.
By then native Indonesian ensembles had toured the West; furthermore, several American universities had added ethnomusicology to
their curriculum (in some cases over the strong objections of scholars
unwilling to extend music's borders beyond the European traditions).

McPhee returned to the USA in 1939. He continued to compose,
although not with the Indonesian flavour of *Tabuh-tabuhan*.
His creative energies seem to have peaked during the time of his
Indonesian involvement; friends from his later years, including
Benjamin Britten, remarked on his frequent fits of depression and
his need to sponge off others in his circle. He wrote and lectured
extensively about his Balinese discoveries, and from 1958 until his
death in 1964 worked at the Institute of Ethnomusicology at the
University of California in Los Angeles, which had been founded
largely as a result of his influence. That institution was the first
American school to build and maintain its own gamelan, created by
McPhee and his ethnomusicologist colleague, Mantle Hood.

By the 1960s, other American composers had looked into the
potential of infusing their own music with the sound and spirit of the
gamelan. Chief among them was the Oregon-born Lou Harrison
(1917–2003), who had worked with Cage on experiments with
percussion music, under the paternal eye of Henry Cowell. Moving
south from his native Portland, Harrison took classes at San Francisco
State College and studied with Cowell in 1934–5. Cowell brought
him together with Cage, and the two worked on a repertory of pieces
for percussion, which they presented (sometimes alone, sometimes
with dancers) throughout California, usually eliciting a strong
audience reaction, some of it enthusiastic, some of it less favourable.

Like Cowell and Cage, Harrison felt little urge to acquire a
background in European traditions. Like Cage, however, Harrison
did move to Los Angeles for a time to acquire an overview of

Lou Harrison, above (photographed in 1977), brought an infusion of Indonesian music into his own works and instructed American students in gamelan. In this gamelan, left, named 'Si Betty' after the patron and photographer Betty Freeman, Harrison is seated second from left.

European rigours in Arnold Schoenberg's classes. As with Cage, not much of the Schoenberg aura remained with Harrison for very long; Harrison's natural bent was towards the creation of elegant and immediately memorable melody, a quality not always congruent with the Schoenbergian note-row.

Long before he had actually visited the Orient, Harrison set about devising instrumental sonorities – and sometimes new instruments – to reproduce the sounds of the gamelan and, thus, to provide composers with a sound resource for their own transcultural compositions. The 'nuclear gamelan' in McPhee's *Tabuh-tabuhan* had suggested the possibility of cloning the sounds of gamelan using Western instruments; the 'junkyard' percussion ensembles that Harrison and Cage designed were intended to do just that. Moreover, Harrison's own music for these ensembles seemed to duplicate the simple, somewhat naive elegance of the authentic Balinese melodies.

In New York (1943–53) Harrison won the admiration of Virgil Thomson, who gave him a job as assistant critic on the *Herald-Tribune*. He also edited several works of Charles Ives – whose musical outlook one would imagine to be very different from Harrison's own – and conducted the world première of Ives's Third Symphony in 1947, nearly half a century after its creation.

From the start of his career, Harrison showed little patience with the notion of following a single stylistic ideal. By the 1950s he seemed committed to an eclectic musical existence; the creative spirit who had eagerly surveyed everything in the world made his own selections and was ready to make them work for him. By the time Harrison had experience of an authentic gamelan, he had already incorporated the sounds and rhythms of this exotic musical ensemble into own music, along with other gadgets he had designed or collected – pianos with tacks embedded in the hammers to heighten their percussive qualities, a set of tuned flowerpots, etc. – that further served to bridge the old East–West gap. Not incidentally, many of his vocal works use texts in Esperanto, the invented, eclectic language that seeks a similar smooth blend of the world's principal languages.

Back in California in 1953, Harrison intensified his explorations into Asian music, at first following Colin McPhee's idea of the 'nuclear gamelan' to imitate the exotic timbres with Western instruments. One of his first works to achieve widespread attention, the

Suite for Piano, Violin and Small Orchestra which Leopold
Stokowski recorded, includes two (of six) movements titled, simply,
Gamelan but scored for ordinary Western instruments plus 'tack-
piano'. Their simple, open sonorities and their accompaniment
figures, obsessively repeating, do indeed capture the essence of the
'honeyed thunder' (as Harrison put it) of a Balinese ensemble.

By 1961 Harrison had moved a step further in his quest for the
East–West musical hybrid. He visited the Orient for the first time in
that year, on a scholarship from the Rockefeller Foundation, and the
trip inspired him to enhance his transcultural leanings by taking on
the task of designing and building (with his longtime associate, the
sculptor William Colvig) authentic gamelans. On his return he began
a teaching career at several California schools, propounding his own
brand of eclecticism – the gospel of the hybrid – to the point where
American composition students studied, constructed and composed
for ensembles that were close approximations of the Indonesian
gamelans. It was a wonderful sight, at the various West Coast schools
where he taught, to watch Harrison sitting with a typical group of

Lou Harrison (left), seated
at the medieval European
droning-drum, and his
partner Bill Colvig, who
built the instruments for
Harrison's gamelans

bleached-blond, suntanned Californian students, creating their own counterparts of a musical culture half a world away.

The implications of Harrison's musical spectrum defined a new world of sonority: a Western composer, student of Schoenberg and Ives, writing for non-Western performance paraphernalia. More deeply, they reinforced Edgard Varèse's notion, already expressed in the 1920s, that Western composers could with impunity turn away from traditional harmonic practice and devise their own eclectic systems. As composers the world over sought out new expressive means, disenchantment with accepted musical systems and a return to certain realities from music's distant past became obsessive in many circles, and found expression in many forms. In Harrison's case, it revealed itself in a return to the system of tuning known as 'just' intonation, which had been the prevailing mode in the music of the Renaissance and early Baroque, before the adoption of equal temperament.

With the formulation of equal temperament early in the eighteenth century, the twelve-note scale, on which all Western melody and harmony is based, became established as the result of compromises, alterations in the 'pure' ratios between the vibration frequencies of related notes (e.g., 3:2 for the interval of the fifth) that would allow composers to write in all keys and to move freely from one to another. Part of Johann Sebastian Bach's purpose in his famous *Well-Tempered Clavier*, consisting of preludes and fugues in all conceivable keys, was to provide examples of composition in all keys. The principle of Classical form, brought to exquisite fruition in the instrumental works of Mozart and Haydn, enriched in the nineteenth century and still honoured (if only in the breach) in the twentieth, also depended on these 'impurities', which allowed the composer to move freely from one key to another, while compromising the 'pure' intervals that had been formulated as far back as Pythagoras.

Composers in this century have made numerous attempts to return to the older, 'purer' intervals; by doing so, however, they forfeit the chance to employ traditional Western harmony. Harrison advocated the return of music to 'just' intonation, the system of pure acoustic intervals most commonly employed by composers up until the time of equal temperament. In his gamelan-inspired music, and to an even greater extent in other works that seem to invoke the harmonic practice of fifteenth- and sixteenth-century polyphony in

Europe, Harrison seems to have reaffirmed the 'purity' of the bygone harmonic systems (together with the vast resources of exotic systems, such as Indonesia's Pelog and Slendro scales, whose tunings once again have nothing to do with the compromises of Western systems). Again, the result has been a repertory of musical hybrids, as Harrison admitted: a choral setting of texts by the Greek poet C. P. Cavafy, sung in Esperanto and accompanied by a gamelan; a concerto for the jazz pianist Keith Jarrett, with the piano tuned in 'just' intonation against the orchestra's equal temperament; a *Pacifika Rondo*, with an orchestra mixing Asian and Western instruments, and a mixture of styles spread through the piece that includes Korean, Japanese and Chinese court music, some Mexican and Spanish colonial music, one or two intrusions of what Harrison calls 'common Atlantic modernism', and even a twelve-note passage or two 'where the listener is least likely to suspect them'. Taking off from Colin McPhee's earlier example, Harrison also created an extensive repertory of original pieces both for 'authentic' Indonesian-style gamelan and for less exotic percussion assemblages that imitate its sound; the ethereal *Concerto in Slendro*, for an ensemble including violin, keyboards and an 'American gamelan' of percussion instruments is worth investigation by anyone seeking immersion in the sounds of other worlds.

Harrison was not alone in his obsession with non-Western musical styles and ancient tuning systems. Another American composer, Alan Hovhaness (born 1911), has consistently evoked his own Armenian ancestral music in his works, a voluminous legacy including some fifty symphonies. Their musical language is basically a conservative one, deriving much from the more garish repertoire of late-Romantic Russian composers, but often spiced with the long, sinuous melodic lines and rhapsodic rhythms of Middle-Eastern song and dance, and with the occasional use of traditional Asian instruments to expand the range of tuning.

Junior to these, La Monte Young (born 1935) has proved himself even more adept in pursuing his innovations in the full glare of the public spotlight. A native of Idaho, Young attended classes in a number of California colleges, where – a small, rabbit-like creature with enormous ideas – he would terrorize audiences with such impromptu 'happenings' as standing up in mid-concert and brushing his teeth. The rumour that he was awarded fellowship money from

Alan Hovhaness's ancestry is an unlikely mix of Scots and Armenian, but the latter element is the more apparent in his music.

La Monte Young (left, in
1971 with Pandit Pran Nath
and Marian Zazeela):
Indian ragas play an
important role in his own
meditative music.

the University of California just to get him off campus has never
been denied.

But La Monte Young was made of sterner stuff. He studied
composition with Karlheinz Stockhausen at Darmstadt, where he
also first discovered the music of John Cage. In New York, where he
lived from 1961, he founded a workshop called The Theatre of
Eternal Music, where he worked on his own music, often abetted by
the visual experiments of the painter and light-show artist Marian
Zazeela, whom he married in 1963. Visitors to his studios were
encouraged to move around the exotically-decorated space, so that
the sine waves generated by electronic equipment around the room
created a constantly changing sound environment. In 1970 he
became a disciple of the Indian composer and vocalist Pandit Pran
Nath, whose native styles began to infiltrate his own work.

By then Young had a distinctive style of his own, which attracted
both admirers and large foundation grants. Some of his music
suggested the remembered sounds from an Idaho boyhood: insects,
motors, and sometimes just the resonance from valleys, lakes and
plains; some reached out in more abstract directions. His music
began to attract many friends and enemies; much of his most notorious work consisted of single sustained chords, which might last

anything from between two hours to a week. The simply titled *Composition 1961*, which is among his best-known consisted entirely of the instruction 'draw a straight line and follow it'. Another piece consists of nothing but a fire, to be built in front of, and appreciated by, the audience.

Probably his most familiar piece is his own triumphant affirmation of the pure if disturbing beauty of 'just' intonation, a work called *The Well-Tuned Piano*, lasting (at least in the recorded version) exactly five hours. Young acquired a superlative exemplar of the Imperial Bösendorfer, the top of the line from that distinguished Austrian piano factory, tuned it in 'just' intonation exactly in keeping with the pure intervals obtainable from a hypothetical E-flat fundamental note ten octaves below the keyboard range, and wired it for sound reproduction. The work itself can be viewed as a continuous meditation across a flood of images. It is fully notated, with individual 'movements' sometimes lasting less than a minute and bearing intricate identifications such as *The Premonition of the Theme of The Lyre of Orpheus Variation of The Goddess of The Caverns under The Pool.* Hearing the work properly is possible only by disconnecting oneself with the expectations of classical harmonies such as Imperial Bösendorfers are wont to produce. Freely associating, one hears instead virtually the entire range of worldwide musical experience, gamelan decidedly included.

Of all American pioneers who have struggled to break out of the imprisoning restrictions of Western harmony, none struggled harder, or with more colourful results, than the California-born Harry Partch (1901–74). The son of apostate missionary parents, Partch grew up in Arizona, where by the age of six he had already mastered several instruments: reed organ, harmonica, cornet and violin among them. His musical education was gleaned from readings in public libraries and by associating with native American Indians in nearby villages; he once listed his influences as 'Yaqui Indians, Chinese lullabies and music-hall songs, Christian and Hebrew hymns, Congo puberty rites … and Mussorgsky's *Boris Godunov*.'

During his time of self-education the young Partch developed a personal philosophy of Western music which, he decided, had begun to go wrong about the time of the Crusades. By 1928 he had produced the first draft of his *Genesis of a Music*, a massive tome that

Harry Partch instructs Francis Thumm on the altered reed organ 'Chromelodeon' in 1972.

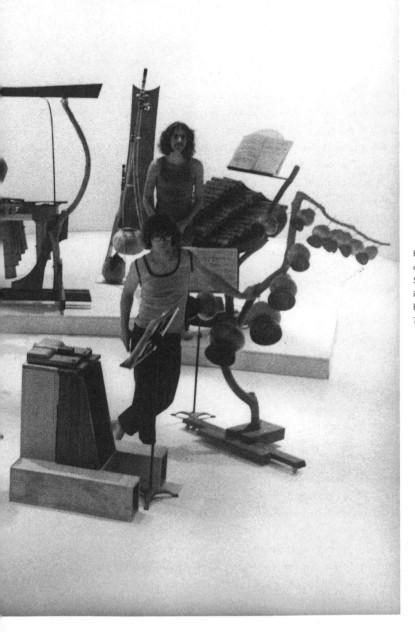

Harry Partch, with members
of his ensemble at San Diego
State University, rehearsing
in 1972 on the instruments
he designed in a work called
The Dreamer That Remains

only saw publication twenty years later. In *Genesis* Partch postulated a
scale of forty-three separate notes, a number he came to after inten-
sive study of a wide variety of non-Western and ancient music. To
exemplify the nature of his new system, and to perform the kind of
music it might engender, he devised and built a phenomenal array of
original instruments: percussion for the most part, but involving a
range of sound-producers including metal plates, wooden bars exactly
sized to particular notes of the Partch scale, stone slabs and large glass
bowls and jars liberated from scientific laboratories. The designing of
instruments, Partch preached, was as integral to the 'corporeality' of
the music as was the performance.

The instruments bore names that attested to Partch's own eclectic
outlook: kithara, chromelodeon, diamond marimba, bloboy and
eucal blossom; to these were added drums copied from Zulu, Hindu
and native American sources: a gorgeous collection to watch, and to
hear as well. In his last days, working at a university in San Diego,
Partch supervised the building of new instruments to execute his
latest fantasies. 'The instruments have to be beautiful, and so do the
players', he growled. 'My music can't get across if it's being played by
a bunch of California prune-pickers.' On occasion the ensemble also
included liquor bottles, whose emptying Partch had personally
attended to. (There exists on film a long and serious monologue by
Partch about the resonance qualities of the bottles for several brands
of Scotch whiskey.)

To underscore his unconventional musical manners, Partch chose
a matching lifestyle. He had lived the hobo – or 'California prune-
picker' – existence for several years, mostly in boxcars in railroad
yards, where he also copied down poetry scribbled on the walls by
previous residents. These elicited musical settings: Partch himself, in
his scruffy and untrained voice, reading these desperate and lonely
lyrics while his 'orchestra' surrounded the words with a halo of music
as from another planet. The best of his music comes across as an
absurdist hodgepodge: American folk-tunes often with Partch's own
off-colour texts, against a background of elegant, ravishing sounds
that might be those of a gamelan playing at the gates of Paradise …
'a weirdly effective mixed-media show', as one British critic has put it.

Most of America's musical pioneers absorbed some part of the
established musical traditions before they set out to destroy them.

Partch seemed to have known, almost from the start, where he was heading. Since his instruments were mostly one-of-a-kind, almost always created to perform a specific work, his music did not circulate widely during most of his lifetime, except on recordings. Late in his career, however, word got out. While at the University of Illinois on a research grant the late 1950s, Partch suddenly became a cult darling, thanks to two big works produced by the university: the dance-satire *The Bewitched,* and an evening-long theatrical piece entitled *Revelation in the Courthouse Park,* a large-scale version of Euripides' *The Bacchae,* with Dionysus transformed into a charismatic rock singer, and with a glorious cacophony from the intermingling of a traditional American marching band and an assemblage of Partch's own instruments. Revived and recorded in Philadelphia in 1987, it seems to have sparked a re-evaluation of Partch's musical ideas, and justly so.

Partch never taught anything like a formal composition seminar, but he subsisted on research appointments from a number of American universities and foundations. An authentic eccentric and, quite possibly, genius, he must also be considered the most 'natural' of serious American composers, totally untouched by the surrounding musical world except when he fulminated against it, as he often did.

Harrison, Young and Partch: they are not exactly a matched set, yet the nature of their work and their outlook creates a linkage. All three have concerned themselves with matters of tuning and into-nation; in the compromise-based 'impure' harmonic system that had served music since the time of Bach, they saw an enormous wrong in need of righting. All three had the imagination to move beyond mere nihilistic proclamations; Harrison designed and built his gamelans, Young practically reinvented the piano, Partch created his kitharas and the bloboy. By so doing, they affirmed a heightened involvement in their own music, a human dimension that the abstractions of the nineteenth-century sonatas and concertos did not always afford. Not accidentally, all three composers were born and spent much of their lives on or near the West Coast, facing Asia and the civilizations whose musics had, from their beginnings in pre-history, centred on that kind of heightened human participation.

*I believe that the use of noise to make music will continue and increase
until we reach a music produced with the aid of electrical instruments …
which will make available for musical purposes any and all sounds that
can be heard. The present methods of writing music, principally those
which employ harmony and its reference to particular steps in the field of
sound, will be inadequate for the composer, who will be faced with the
entire field of sound.*

John Cage, in *Silence*, written,
with extraordinary prophetic clarity, in 1937

Electronic music became a reality shortly after World War I, when
the Russian acoustician and composer Leon Theremin pioneered
the instrument that bore his name. Edgard Varèse was one of the
serious composers, anxious to expand the musical language beyond
the confines of the traditional scales, who took the instrument
seriously for a time, and who originally scored two theremins into
his *Ecuatorial* of 1932. The theremin eventually made its way to
Hollywood, where for half a century it has been a prime source for
the other-worldly sounds demanded by mystery and science-fiction
films (starting with Alfred Hitchcock's classic *Spellbound*).

It was the development of tape-recording, immediately after World
War II, that brought the idea of electronically produced sound onto
the musical scene. Composers could now not only produce sounds
through oscillators modified by filters, reverberation devices and the
growing range of sound-control devices; they could also put these
sounds onto tape, where they could be edited, installed in repeating
tape-loop patterns, combined with other sounds in counterpoint and,
in short, present the composer with a resource so vast as to make all
previous sound-producing apparatus – even the symphony orchestra
– seem but a crude beginning. The further refinement of sound-
producing devices, including equipment that could synthesize with
impressive verisimilitude the sounds of acoustic instruments, further
broadened the horizons. The concomitant craze for science fiction
further enhanced the staying power of the new musical gadgetry.
The 1956 film *Forbidden Planet*, an imaginative re-working of
Shakespeare's *The Tempest* set in outer space, was a pioneer in its
use of an entirely electronic musical score.

Today's composers of electronic music can fulfil their needs with
splendidly responsive equipment which will fit onto a desktop.

The first electronic-music studios, however, were far bulkier and
vastly more expensive. In Paris in 1951, with underwriting from
Radiotélévision Française, Pierre Schaeffer and Pierre Henry established a studio where such distinguished composers as Varèse, Pierre
Boulez and Olivier Messiaen were frequent participants. At Cologne
that same year the composer Herbert Eimert created a studio funded
by the Northwest German Radio, where Karlheinz Stockhausen
created his pioneering five-channel *Gesang der Jünglinge* ('Song of
the Holy Children'), combining the singing of a boy soprano –
electronically fragmented, transposed and superimposed upon itself –
with an electronic texture derived from the building up of sine waves,
carefully avoiding any relationship to the 'normal' pitches produced
by traditional instruments.

    The first American electronic studio was founded at the University
of Illinois in 1958, but this was soon to be dwarfed. In New York in
1959 a consortium of supporting institutions, including universities,

the Bell Laboratories and RCA, turned a warehouse at the edge of
Harlem into a state-of-the-art electronic studio. Three major composers, already established among the leading East-Coast progressives,
joined the Columbia-Princeton Electronic Music Center as co-
directors: Milton Babbitt, Otto Luening and Vladimir Ussachevsky.

Babbitt (born 1916) was already established as the apostle of Arnold
Schoenberg's twelve-note methods; his dual backgrounds, as composer and mathematician, furnished him with insights into the
aesthetic nature of Schoenberg's numerical permutations. His own
music, intricate and mathematical, seemed to take the serial techniques of Schoenberg and his disciple Anton Webern onto even more

Milton Babbitt, co-founder of
the Columbia-Princeton
Electronic Music Center in
New York in the 1950s,
shows off its RCA Mark II
Synthesizer, *right*.
Nowadays a mere desktop
computer can produce the
same results as this monster
machine, and much faster.

Pioneer electronic composers Otto Luening (left) and Vladimir Ussachevsky as they appeared in 1952

rarefied levels, in which not only the twelve notes of the tempered
scale, but also such other matters as rhythm and sonority were also set
forth in strictly serialized order ... little revealing the incidental news
that Babbitt, before any of this, had also had a fling as a composer of
popular romantic ballads. In his classes at Princeton University,
Babbitt guided generations of young composers towards an embrace
of serial techniques. The possibilities in electronic music, which he
began to realize early in the 1950s, appealed to the scientist in his soul
no less than the musician.

At Princeton, RCA had established a research centre specifically
aimed at developing sound-synthesizing and computer technology;
Babbitt was attracted to RCA's Mark I synthesizer, and served as a
consultant for the development of the improved Mark II which, in
turn, became the basis for the Columbia-Princeton project in New
York. In 1964 he created *Philomel* for soprano and electronic tape,
using John Hollander's poetic refashioning of the legend of
Philomela, as originally told in Ovid's *Metamorphoses*; it would
become the Columbia-Princeton Center's best-known product. As a
pioneering work in the combination of live music and tape, *Philomel*
remains an early milestone in the annals of electronic music.

Luening (born 1900) and Ussachevsky (1911–90, born in
Manchuria to Russian parents who emigrated to the USA in 1930)
were, similarly, well established as composers and teachers (at New
York's Columbia University) well before the electronic evolution
attracted them. Ussachevsky had been a pupil of Luening, and
the first of their many collaborative projects, consisted of tape-
recording natural and man-made sounds onto tape, which they then
processed. By the mid-1950s, they had discovered the expanded
opportunities in electronically produced sounds. In 1954 their first
major joint work, the *Rhapsodic Variations* for taped sounds and
symphony orchestra, was performed and recorded by the Louisville
Symphony Orchestra.

Hearing this music from what might be called the electronic pre-
history, against the enormous advances made since its time, one is
struck by its relative tameness – a comparison analogous to the
distance between, say, the early symphonies of the Classical period
(Johann Stamitz, say) and the masterpieces of Haydn and Mozart.
For all the novelty of its sound, and the further novelty of its exotic

provenance, much of the first generation of electronic music seemed to stem from the sounds of an old-fashioned electric organ, augmented by an occasional whoosh or clickety-clack from the sound-effects drawer. The electronic music that seemed most attractive to early audiences were such projects as the *Switched-On Bach* recordings, with the engineer/keyboard-player Walter (later Wendy) Carlos, playing works by Bach on the popular synthesizer devised by Robert Moog, adding licks and colouristic effects to the otherwise self-sufficient music but hardly advancing the capabilities of the electronic medium.

Even among composers who clung to more 'natural' sound-producers, the advent of tape made its mark; composers became obsessed with the vast range of possibilities available also from traditional instruments. George Crumb (born 1929) was one of the most successful; his haunting *Ancient Voices of Children*, setting fragments of a García Lorca text, uses an amplified piano, a percussion section which includes tuned stone slabs, and offstage effects; his brilliant set of piano pieces (called *Makrokosmos*, perhaps as a tribute to Béla Bartók's *Mikrokosmos*) again employs amplification to expand the timbral potential of the piano itself.

On the West Coast, already identified as a fertile breeding-ground for experiment in the arts, the San Francisco Tape Music Center, also established in 1959, embodied a far broader view of where the uneasy marriage of art and technology might be heading. Its founders were a group of young composers worthy of the pioneer epithet – among them Morton Subotnick, Pauline Oliveros and Ramon Sender, later Steve Reich and Terry Riley – most of them students of a remarkable experimenter named Robert Erickson (1917–97). In his own music, Erickson had used tape and other processing devices to create musical textures from nature sounds: waves crashing against the California coast, a brook gurgling its way across a meadow in the Sierras. At the Tape Music Center the Erickson alumni carried on his experiments, and they were often joined by progressive figures from other fields: poets, film-makers, visual artists. From this interaction a new term came into the arts: multimedia.

In its time the Tape Music Center served the San Francisco Bay Area as its creative cutting edge. One major philosophical difference between the San Francisco and New York studios might be noted

California electronic
composer Morton Subotnick
seen in 1993 at a grand
piano that also has
been wired to function
as a synthesizer

here: by employing keyboards as a way of articulating their music
synthesizer, the New Yorkers were initially committed to continuing
reference to the major and minor scales. San Francisco's synthesizers,
designed by Donald Buchla (himself a composer), could operate
specific to any desired frequency. Terry Riley and Steve Reich, identified today among the founders of musical minimalism (along with
La Monte Young), created some of their first important works at the
Center: Riley's *In C*, a repetitive work of indeterminate length built
around the note C; Reich's *It's Gonna Rain*, in which a phrase from a

street evangelist's speech is constantly repeated (on stereophonic tape), with the tracks gradually going out of phase with one another and creating an authentic audio downpour.

What seemed to define the difference in creative energy between the two experimental centres is this: New York's multi-million dollar installation flourished in the stern grip of academic and corporate control; San Francisco's shoestring operation delighted in its freedom. (Morton Subotnick recalls that the San Francisco Police were convinced – wrongly – that the Tape Music Center was a drug operation, and so the participants and supporters had to be sworn to keep the address secret.) By 1966 the pioneering spirit was rewarded with a sizeable financial grant from New York's Rockefeller Foundation, but the grant carried the stipulation that the Center need attach itself to a reputable educational institution. Mills College, a nearby institution whose music faculty boasted the presence of the formidable French composer Darius Milhaud, and whose distinguished alumni included not only Subotnick but also the progressive jazzman

O Pioneers! John Cage and Nicolas Slonimsky, ardent proponents of the notion that music must never stand still

Dave Brubeck, was the obvious and proper choice. Saddened by the institutionalization of their free-form baby, but with their innovations now widely hailed and imitated, the founders of the San Francisco Tape Music Center moved on to explore new territories.

Epilogue

If the pioneering spirit of twentieth-century America can boast a connecting thread, that would be the personality and achievements of Nicolas Slonimsky, Los Angeles resident since 1963, world citizen since 1894, a few weeks past his hundredth birthday as these words are written. It was the Russian-born Slonimsky who, mere months after his arrival in the United States, produced first hearings of major works by Ives, Cowell and Varèse, wrote perceptive criticisms of their works in publications worldwide, and was later hailed by Cowell as 'having conducted more works by original Americans than almost any other conductor'. Having done as much as anyone, in his early years, to upset the complacency of the musical world around him, Slonimsky then proceeded to put that world in order: as editor, since 1958, of the *Biographical Dictionary of Musicians* which still loyally bears the name of its nineteenth-century founder, Theodore Baker, and as author of the incredibly thorough day-by-day account of *Music Since 1900*. Like the listings in his encyclopaedias, Slonimsky's own contact with the changing state of music has remained up-to-date; in his 1988 autobiography *Perfect Pitch* he reviews his friendships with the first generation of musical pioneers, and moves on to perceptive considerations of such contemporary innovators as La Monte Young – not to mention the San Francisco composer Charles Amirkhanian, whose fame rests partly on his having created an entire composition by processing taped phrases from some of Slonimsky's classroom lectures into an extensive collage.

It is Slonimsky's own voice, therefore, witty and phenomenally comprehending, that identifies and links the pioneering efforts of this century, in the 2,115 pages of the latest *Baker's*, the 1,260-page *Music Since 1900* (recently published in a brand-new edition that brings the worldwide chronicle up to Christmas Eve 1991), or the more succinct autobiography. Without himself having composed very much of musical significance (although such capricious efforts as his set of songs to texts from print advertisements – e.g., *Children cry for*

Castoria – have their charm), Slonimsky stands forth as the hero among American musical pioneers, the guardian of their memory and chronicler of their significance.

The significance of the pioneers rests, of course, on the followers who moved along the trails they blazed, and extended their span. Naturally it does not always happen that these ancestral trails proceed along straight lines. We can instinctively sense the connections between the eclectic explorations of Lou Harrison, with his fondness for creating an East-meets-West hybrid language, and the patterned repetitiousness of the American minimalists Steve Reich and Philip Glass (who also went abroad to study first-hand the rhythms of African drumming and the gamelans and ragas of Asia). We sense the supple, deceptively soft-spoken patterns of John Cage in the music of his closest disciple, Morton Feldman, most of all in the late Feldman works that can spread mere handfuls of notes and silences across three or four hours and, in a properly dedicated performance, hold an audience motionless.

A direct line extending back to Charles Ives may be more difficult to discern. His own aloofness in the last decades of his life rendered unlikely any approach by a hopeful disciple or successor. Even so, the very fact of those decades of obscurity seemed to smooth the onward path from Ives's own music toward posterity. By the time his music was rediscovered and restored to public awareness – first through the efforts of Slonimsky and Lou Harrison, later through the frenzied evangelism of Leonard Bernstein – the music world was ready to cope with some of the startling devices in such works as *The Unanswered Question* and the *Three Places in New England.*

It is interesting to speculate where our early pioneers might stand in the face of the facilities available to composers today. Charles Ives, with his crusty New England work ethic, would probably be horrified at how easy the computer makes it to crash together several musical thoughts at once; he was the great believer in human sweat. Henry Cowell would be delighted at the possibilities in tape, and would construct huge and wonderful symphonies out of the sounds of brooks and surf – as, indeed, his unacknowledged disciple Robert Erickson did for years in California. Harry Partch would surely reject the notion of electronic gadgetry replacing the improbably beautiful instruments he had built for his music. Edgard Varèse would joyously greet the new technology, while claiming credit for having envisioned it back in Paris in 1913. John Cage lived long enough to study and exploit the new technology, and had already enlisted the aid of the computer in resolving some of his knottier compositional problems.

Yet it is difficult to pinpoint any one American composer today as the direct descendant of any of those pioneering figures. Two who qualify might be Henry Brant, Montreal-born of American parentage in 1913, and therefore contemporary to John Cage, and the Missouri-born James Tenney (born 1934), although both composers' music is still not nearly well enough known.

Brant, who moseys through life wearing a ski suit and a railroader's cap, is a true original. Early on he experimented with the sound potential of assorted kitchen utensils, at the same time exploring the musical possibilities of space. He placed performing groups in widely separated positions in large halls or outdoor spaces. One of his best-known works, called *Angels and Devils* – available in a recording – is composed for a solo flute and an orchestra consisting only of more flutes, and it sounds as spaced-out and raucous as the description suggests. Another work, *5-&-10-cent Store Music*, scored for violin, piano and kitchen hardware, takes no account of its bizarre instru-mentation and achieves a remarkably lyrical intensity.

Early studies with Eduard Steuermann, a close associate of Arnold Schoenberg, gave James Tenney an insight into systematic European atonality. Later he worked at the pioneering electronic studio at the University of Illinois; later still, with Varèse, Partch and Cage. In the 1970s he discovered and wrote about the hitherto obscure music of the American expatriate Conlon Nancarrow, who in his studio in Mexico City had invented a way of creating immensely complex music by punching holes into the paper rolls of a player-piano, thus creating through this primitive technology the same subtle motoric variety that Henry Cowell had attempted with his Rhythmicon decades earlier. At the same time Tenney's experiments with tuning systems provided a kinship with the works of Lou Harrison and La Monte Young. Only a single work of Tenney's is currently available on disc, as part of a variorum on the enterprising Mode label; with luck, that situation could change.

Developments in the design of electronic instruments – the syn-thesizer, able to produce credible imitations of both conceivable and inconceivable musical timbres, and the sampler, capable of processing any given sound (noise, a human voice, an acoustic instrument) – brought much of this technology within reach of a fledgling composer's budget. By the 1980s the computers to access, manipulate and organize these sounds had also been priced down to affordable limits. Any educational institution could now afford the modest funds to install some kind of computer-music laboratory; most students could also duplicate these facilities in home studios. Morton Subotnick, who in the 1960s had created large-scale electronic pieces to be 'published' on long-playing records (e.g., *Silver Apples of the Moon, The Wild Bull,* both underwritten and produced by Nonesuch Records), inaugurated the 1990s with an electronic work to be performed interactively on a compact disc through a Macintosh computer, with the consumer making choices as to the sequence and nature of the musical components and the images that accompanied them on the screen.

As the century nears its end, the very nature of music has seemed under challenge; yet that had always been the case. The sons of J. S. Bach found their father's music outmoded, and abandoned Baroque counterpoint for the serene orderliness of Classicism. Richard Wagner found the aesthetic of his time confining, and proposed a new view of the 'total art work' in which all expressive arts would combine into a glorious mix. The delight in impurity that allowed Charles Ives to stir popular marches and hymns into his symphonies and string quartets also motivates today's new-music purveyors, the Kronos String Quartet, to include their own versions of Jimi Hendrix and Thelonious Monk pieces on their concert programmes, alongside other works of more serious mien. 'Cherish the hybrid', Lou Harrison urged, and history has borne him out.

It is a further axiom in the arts that matters tend to come around full circle. The Classical era, which began with the abjuration of Baroque counterpoint, culminated in the five-part counterpoint at the end of Mozart's last symphony and the great oratorios of Haydn. Earlier in our own century the schism between the neo-classicism of Igor Stravinsky and Schoenbergian atonality was breached when, after Schoenberg's death, Stravinsky began to compose in the atonal style. In more recent years other composers seem to be rummaging music's distant past and rediscovering what remains relevant in bygone musical languages: hence the infusion of neo-medievalism in the works of the mysticism-inspired Arvo Pärt and Henryk Górecki, or the overt romantic lushness in the music of George Rochberg – who once actually recanted in so many words his former abstruse musical styles – or the neo-romantic David del Tredici, now proceeding headlong along kinder, gentler paths.

It is usually difficult to recognize a true act of pioneering at the moment of its inception. Charles Ives's footsteps remained unfollowed for decades after he initiated his unorthodox musical practices. Edgard Varèse's music circulated among a small group of connoisseurs, until a few musicians – notably Pierre Boulez – took up his cause. Cowell and Cage await their deserved acclaim; Harry Partch's music slowly achieves recognition. The 'pioneers' of electronic music, like the die-hard serialists around Milton Babbitt, earn their fame bit by bit, even as some of their electronic discoveries have begun to ooze into pop-music areas.

Beginning in the 1980s, there has been something of a reaction against the grittier aspects of the vast spectrum of pioneering music. The American composer George Rochberg writes string quartets incorporating passages that might pass for Schubert or Mahler outtakes; the Pulitzer laureate David del Tredici writes a series of tone poems inspired by *Alice's Adventures in Wonderland* that might pass for Richard Strauss. It could be, of course, that these seeming throwbacks are actually the next generation of pioneers. Stranger things have happened.

Some audiences react in relief at the suggestion that composers are now turning away from the abrasive pioneering activities in America's musical past; some audiences still sneak out of concert halls at the playing of Igor Stravinsky's *Rite of Spring*, first introduced in 1913 but still a pioneering act. Others, however, choose to remain.

Alan Rich
Los Angeles, 1995

Selective List of Works

The following is an essential summary of major or representative works by the composers treated here, with dates of composition and first performance ('fp'). The composers are listed alphabetically and their works ordered chronologically, within specified categories where appropriate. In many cases the dates of first performance are impossible to ascertain accurately, since premières often took place under informal circumstances; this is especially true in the case of the (literally) hundreds of small, experimental works by Henry Cowell and John Cage which are therefore marked 'fp?'

Milton Babbitt

Composition for Twelve Instruments (1948, revised 1954) fp?

Philomel, for soprano and tape, text by John Hollander (1964). fp New York, 1964

Relata II (1968). fp New York, 16 January 1969

Concerto for Violin, Small Orchestra and Synthesized Tape (1974). fp New York, 13 March 1976

A Solo Requiem, for soprano and pianists, texts by Shakespeare, Hopkins, Meredith, Stramm, Dryden (1977). fp New York, 10 February 1979

String Quartet No. 5 (1982). fp Los Angeles, 1982

Piano Concerto (1985). fp New York, 19 January 1986

Earle Brown

Octet I, for eight tapes (1952-53). fp?

Octet II, for eight tapes (1957). fp?

Available Forms I, for eighteen instruments (1961). fp?

Available Forms II, for large orchestra with two conductors (1962). fp?

Calder Piece, for four percussionists, mobile (1963). fp Valencia, California, 9 March 1980

Modules I–II, for orchestra (1966); *III* (1969). fp?

Sounder Rounds, for orchestra (1982). fp Saarbrucken, 12 May 1983

Tracer, for six instruments, four-track tape (1984). fp Berlin, 8 February 1985

John Cage

Trio for Percussion (1936). fp Santa Monica, 9 December 1938

First Construction (in Metal), for six percussionists (1939). fp Seattle, 9 December 1939

Second Construction, for four percussionists (1940). fp Portland, Oregon, 14 February 1940

Third Construction, for four percussionists (1941). fp San Francisco, 14 May 1941

The City Wears a Slouch Hat, radio play with text by Kenneth Patchen (1942). fp (broadcast) Chicago, 31 May 1942

The Wonderful Widow of Eighteen Springs, for voice and piano, text by James Joyce (1942). fp New York, 5 March 1942

Amores, for prepared pianos and percussion (1943).
fp New York, 7 February 1943

The Perilous Night, for prepared piano (1944). fp New
York, 5 April 1944

Three Dances, for amplified prepared piano (1944–5).
fp New York, 21 January 1945

Sonatas and Interludes for Prepared Piano (1946–8).
fp Black Mountain, North Carolina, spring 1948

String Quartet (1949–50). fp?

Imaginary Landscape No. 4, for twelve radios (1951).
fp New York, 2 May 1951

4 '33 ", for any instruments (1952). fp Woodstock, New
York, 29 August 1959

Williams Mix, for eight one-track and four two-track
tapes (1952). fp Urbana, IL, 22 March 1953

Music for Piano, 1–84 (1953–6). fp?

Concert for Piano and Orchestra (1957–8). fp New
York, 15 May 1958

Atlas Eclipticalis, for any ensemble from eighty-six
instruments (1961). fp Montreal, 3 August 1961

Variations II–VII; anybody doing anything (1961–6).
fpp, New York, Los Angeles, Washington 1961–6

HPSCHD, for amplified harpsichord and fifty-one
tapes (1967–9). fp Urbana, IL, 16 May 1969

Song Books, solos for voice 3–92 (1970). fp Paris,
26 October 1970

Études Australes, for piano (1974–5). fp New York,
25 January 1975 (excerpts); Witten, Germany, 25 April
1982 (complete)

Lecture on the Weather, for instruments, voices,
tapes, film, texts by Thoreau (1975). fp Toronto,
26 February 1976

Apartment House, Renga, for seventy-eight
instruments, voices, mixed media (1976). fp Boston,
29 September 1976

Quartets I–VII, for up to ninety-six instruments
(1976). fp Bonn, 9 December 1977

Freeman Études, for violin (1977–80). fp Books
I and II: New York, 24 April 1978, Books III and IV:
Zürich, 26 June 1991

A Dip in the Lake: Dances and Marches, for
performers, listeners and records (1978). fp before
May 1978

Roaratorio, an Irish Circus on *Finnegans Wake*,
text by James Joyce (1979). fp Donaueschingen,
20 October 1979

Thirty Pieces for String Quartet (1983). fp Darmstadt,
27 July 1984

Music for —, for instrumental ensemble (1984–5).
fp New Milford (Connecticut), 15 August 1984

Etcetera, for two to four orchestras and tape (1986).
fp Tokyo, 8 December 1986

Europeras 1 and 2; for nineteen singers and
operatic performing forces (1988). fp Frankfurt,
12 December 1987

One, Two, Four, Five, Seven; for various instrumental
combinations (1988). fp?

Europeras 3 and 4, for singers, piano, phonographs
(1989). fp London, 17 June 1990

Eight, for mixed ensemble (1991). fp?

Europera 5, for pianist, two singers, tape (1991).
fp Buffalo, 18 April 1991

Henry Cowell

Orchestral

Sinfonietta, for chamber orchestra (1928). fp Boston,
28 April 1928

Concerto for Piano and Orchestra (1928).
fp (complete), Havana, 28 December 1930

Reel, for small orchestra (1928). fp New York,
17 May 1933

Synchrony (1930). fp Paris, 6 June 1931

Symphony No. 2, 'Anthropos' (1938). fp Brooklyn,
9 March 1941

Old American Country Set (1939). fp Indianapolis,
28 February 1940

Hymn and Fuguing Tune No. 3, for strings (1944).
fp Los Angeles, 14 April 1951

Symphony No. 4, 'Short Symphony' (1946). fp Boston,
24 October 1946

Symphony No. 5 (1948). fp Washington,
5 January 1949

Symphony No. 11, 'Seven Rituals' (1953). fp Louisville,
29 May 1954

Symphony No. 12 (1955–6). fp Houston,
28 March 1960

Persian Set (1957). fp Tehran, 17 September 1957

Symphony No. 13, 'Madras' (1956–8). fp Madras,
3 March 1959

Stage Works

Music for Creation Dawn, twenty-seven incidental
pieces (1913). fp Carmel, California, 16 August 1913

The Building of Bamba, Irish mythological
opera, libretto by Varian (1917). fp Halcyon, California,
7 August 1930

Les Mariés de la Tour Eiffel, incidental music to the play
by Jean Cocteau (1939). fp Seattle, 24 March 1939

A Full Moon in March, dance (1950). fp Fargo, North
Dakota, 1 December 1950

Chamber/Instrumental

String Quartet No. 1, 'Pedantic' (1915–16). fp?

Quartet Romantic, for two flutes, violin and viola
(1915–17). fp?

Quartet Euphometric, for string quartet (1916–19). fp?

Ostinato pianissimo, for piano and four percussion
(1934). fp?

String Quartet No. 2 (1934). fp?

String Quartet No. 3, Mosaic Quartet (1935). fp?

String Quartet No. 4, United Quartet (1936). fp?

Twenty-six Simultaneous Mosaics, for clarinet,
percussion, piano, violin and cello (1964). fp?

Piano/Vocal

Over 500 pieces, 1910–65, including (for piano):
Anger Dance (1914), *Exultation* (1919), *Voice of Lir*
(1919), *Vestiges* (1920), *Snows of Fujiyama* (1922),
The Hero Sun (1922), *Aeolian Harp* (1923), *Harp of
Life* (1924), *Lilt of the Reel* (1925), *The Banshee*
(1925), *Maestoso* (1929), *Rhythmicana* (1938),
Hilarious CurtainOpener (1939), *Hymn and Fuguing
Piece* (1943), *Mountain Music* (1944)

George Crumb

Ancient Voices of Children, for soprano, boy soprano, ensemble, electric piano, toy piano, percussion, text by Federico García Lorca (1970). fp Washington, 31 October 1970

Vox balaenae, for three masked musicians (1971). fp Washington, 17 March 1972

Makrokosmos I and II, for amplified piano (1973–4). fp New York, 8 February 1973, 12 November 1974

Morton Feldman

Durations I–IV, for solo instruments (1960–61). fp?

The King of Denmark, for percussion (1964). fp?

The Viola in My Life, for viola and orchestra (1970). fp London, 19 September 1970

Rothko Chapel, for soprano, alto, chorus and instruments (1971). fp Houston, April 1972

For Frank O'Hara, for instrumental ensemble (1973). fp New York, December 1973

Three Voices, for solo voice and tape (1982). fp Valencia, California, March 1983

For Philip Guston, for chamber ensemble (1984). fp New York, 21 April 1985

For Samuel Beckett, for chamber ensemble (1986). fp Amsterdam, 12 June 1987

Lou Harrison

Concerto in Slendro (1961). fp?

Lo Koro Sutro, for chorus and ensemble, text in Esperanto (1972). fp?

Double Concerto, for violin, cello and gamelan (1981–2). fp?

Piano Concerto (1985). fp 30 January 1986

Varied Trio, for violin, piano and percussion (1986). fp Oakland, California, 14 May 1987

Charles Ives

Orchestral/Band

Holiday Quickstep, for piccolo, two cornets, two violins and piano (December 1887). fp Danbury, Connecticut, 16 January 1888

Symphony No. 1 (1895–8). fp Washington, 26 April 1953

Symphony No. 2 (1898). fp New York, 22 February 1951

Symphony No. 3, 'The Camp Meeting' (1904). fp New York, 5 April 1946

Set for Theatre or Chamber Orchestra (1906–11). fp Danbury, February 1932

Two Contemplations: *The Unanswered Question, Central Park in the Dark* (1906). fp New York, 11 May 1946

Washington's Birthday (1909). fp San Francisco, 3 September 1931

The Gong on the Hook and Ladder (?1911). fp New York, 21 January 1967

Robert Browning Overture (1908–12). fp New York, October 1963

First Orchestral Set: *Three Places in New England* (1908–14). fp New York, 10 January 1931

Decoration Day (1912). fp Havana, December 1931

The Fourth of July (1911–13). fp Paris, 21 February 1932

Symphony No. 4 (1909–16). fp New York,
26 April 1965

Chamber

String Quartet No. 1 (1896). fp New York,
24 April 1957

Trio, for violin, cello, piano (1902–3). fp Berea, Ohio,
24 May 1948

Hallowe'en, for string quartet and piano (1906). fp San
Francisco, 28 May 1934

Largo risoluto, 'as to the Law of Diminishing Returns'
(1906). fp New York, 19 February 1965

Violin Sonata No. 1 (1902–8). fp New York,
31 March 1946

Violin Sonata No. 2 (1907–10). fp 18 March 1924

String Quartet No. 2 (1911–13). fp Saratoga Springs,
New York, 15 September 1946

Violin Sonata No. 3 (1913–14). fp Los Angeles,
16 March 1942

Violin Sonata No. 4, 'Children's Day at the Camp
Meeting' (1906–16). fp New York, 14 January 1940

Piano

The Anti-Abolitionist Riots; Some Southpaw Pitching,
studies (1908). fp New York, 3 April 1950

Piano Sonata No. 1 (1901–9). fp New York,
17 February 1949

Piano Sonata No. 2, 'Concord, Mass., 1840–60'
(1910–15). fp New York, 20 January 1939

Three Quarter-Tone Pieces, for two pianos (1903–24).
fp New York, 14 February 1924

Vocal

Psalm Settings: xxiv, liv, lxvii, xc, cl (1894). fp?

Psalm settings: xiv, xxv, c, cxxxv (1899–1901). fp?

Song: *General William Booth Enters Into Heaven*, text
by Vachel Lindsay (1914). fp?

Song: *Charlie Rutlage*, text by D. J. O'Malley
(1921). fp?

Otto Luening

Music for Orchestra (1923). fp New York, 26 May 1978

Kentucky Concerto (1951). fp Louisville, 9 March 1951

Sonority Forms II (1983). fp Bennington Vt.,
4 June 1983

Evangeline, opera (1930–48). fp New York, 5 May 1948

Collaborations with Vladimir Ussachevsky

Rhapsodic Variations, for tape and orchestra(1954).
fp Louisville, 20 March 1954

Poem in Cycles and Bells, for tape and orchestra (1954).
fp Los Angeles, 18 November 1954

Concerted Piece, for tape and orchestra (1960). fp New
York, 10 March 1960

Colin McPhee

Balinese Ceremonial Music, for two pianos
(1934–8). fp?

Tabuh-tabuhan, for large orchestra (1936). fp Mexico City, 4 September 1936

Harry Partch

Yankee Doodle Fantasy, for soprano, flexatone, tin flute, oboe (1941). fp?

The Bewitched, for solo voice and instruments (1952–5). fp Urbana, Illinois, 26 March 1957

Oedipus, incidental music to the Sophocles play (1952). fp Oakland, California, 14 March 1952

Revelation in the Courthouse Park (after Euripides), for sixteen solo voices and large ensemble (1960). fp Urbana, Illinois 11 April 1962

Delusion of the Fury (1965–6). fp Los Angeles, 9 January 1969

Terry Riley

In C (1964). fp San Francisco, 21 May 1965

Descending Moonshine Dervishes, for electronic organ (1975). fp?

Salome Dances for Peace, for string quartet (1989). fp?

Edgard Varèse

Amériques, for orchestra (1918–21). fp Philadelphia, 9 April 1926. Revised 1927; fp Paris, 30 May 1929

Offrandes, for soprano and small orchestra, texts by V. Huidobro and J . J. Tablada (1921). fp 23 April 1922

Hyperprism, for nine winds and seven percussion (1922–3). fp New York, 4 March 1928

Octandre, for winds, brass, double bass (1923). fp New York, 13 January 1924

Intégrales, for eleven winds and four percussion (1924–5). fp New York, 1 March 1925

Arcana, for orchestra (1925–7). fp Philadelphia, 8 April 1927

Ionisation, for thirteen percussion (1929–31). fp New York, 6 March 1933

Ecuatorial, for bass solo, unison chorus, eight brass, piano, organ, ondes martenots, six percussion, text from Popol Yuy of Maya Quiché (1932–4). fp 15 April 1934

Density 21.5, for flute (1936). fp 16 February 1936

Étude pour espace, for chorus, two pianos and percussion (1947). fp New York, 23 February 1947

Déserts, for fourteen winds, piano, five percussion and two-track tape (1950–54). fp Paris, 2 December 1954

La procession de Vergès, tape for film on Joan Miró (1955)

Poème électronique, three-track tape (1958). fp Brussels, 2 May 1958

Nocturnal, for singers, chorus and small orchestra, text by Anaïs Nin (1961). fp (incomplete) 1 May 1961. Completed by Chou Wen-chung (1973)

Christian Wolff

Music for Merce Cunningham, for chamber ensemble (1959). fp?

For 5 or 10 People, for any instruments (1962). fp?

Dark as a Dungeon, for various instruments (1977). fp?

Rock About (Starving to Death on a Government Claim), for violin and viola (1980). fp?

I Like to Think of Harriet Tubman, for female voices (1984). fp?

La Monte Young

Vision, for eleven instruments (1959). fp?

Piano Pieces for David Tudor Nos. 1–3 (1960). fp?

Death Chant, for male chorus, carillon, large bells (1961). fp?

The Second Dream of the High-tension Line Stepdown Transformer, any instruments capable of sustaining groups of four notes in just intonation (1962). fp?

The Well-Tuned Piano (1964–81). fp 3 June 1974

Map of 49's Dream the Two Systems of Eleven Sets of Galactic Intervals Ornamental Lightyears Tracery (1966). fp?

Further Reading

John Cage

There is as yet no definitive biography of Cage, although several are in preparation; David Revill's *The Roaring Silence* is compiled from hearsay, although the history and musical descriptions are generally reliable. But the enormous written legacy of Cage himself makes amends: the collections of essays (*Silence, X, A Year from Monday* and *From the Birds*); the Norton Lectures (called, simply *I–VI*) are set as mesostics and not easily read, but there is a continuously-running footnote consisting of questions from students (some of them obviously baffled). The New York writer Richard Kostelanetz (nephew of the pop-concert conductor) has collected several volumes of interviews with Cage and miscellaneous essays; they too are valuable, and the juxtaposition of the names of Cage and Kostelanetz forms a delicious irony.

Cage, J. *Silence* (Middletown, Conn., Wesleyan University Press, 1961; London, Marion Boyars, 1973)

Diary: Part III (New York, Something Else Press, 1967)

A Year from Monday (Middletown, Conn., Wesleyan University Press, 1967; London, Marion Boyars, 1985)

Diary: Part IV (New York, S.M.S. Press, 1968)

Notations (New York, Something Else Press, 1969)

M (Middletown, Wesleyan University Press, 1973)

Kostelanetz, R. The American Avant-garde, Part II: John Cage', *Stereo Review,* xxii/5 (1969), 61; reprinted in *Master Minds* (New York, Macmillan, 1969)

Revill, D. *The Roaring Silence* (New York, Arcade Publishing; London, Bloomsbury, 1992)

Henry Cowell

No proper biography of Cowell exists. The valuable collection of essays that he edited in 1933, *American Composers on American Music* (reprinted in 1962 by Ungar) contains Nicolas Slonimsky's biographical essay (along with Cowell's essay on Ives); the 1962 revision extends only to the preface. Slonimsky's chapter on Cowell, 'Jailed Friend', in his autobiography *Perfect Pitch* (New York, Oxford University Press, 1988) is valuable if factually flawed. Michael Hicks's full account of Cowell's arrest and imprisonment appears in the Spring 1991 issue of JAMS, the Journal of the American Musicological Society.

Charles Ives

The major sources for Ives's own writing are the *Essays Before a Sonata* – published privately by Ives in 1920, now available in the Dover paperback (with essays by Debussy and Busoni) – and the 'Memos', which the pianist and scholar John Kirkpatrick collated, edited and annotated. *Charles Ives and His Music*, by the Cowells is a loving portrait but brief and often factually inaccurate; David Wooldridge's *From the Steeples and Mountains: a Study of Charles Ives* is of negligible value. Better than either of these is Frank Rossiter's *Charles Ives and His America* and the more general but valuable *Music in a New-Found Land* by Britain's steadfast Americophile, Wilfrid Mellers. Nicolas Slonimsky's autobiography, written at the age of ninety-four, is full of valuable Ivesiana, and would be required reading even if it were not.

Cowell, H. and S. R. Cowell, *Charles Ives and His Music* (New York, Oxford University Press, 1955, revised 1969; New York, Da Capo, 1983)

Ives, C. E. 'Essays Before a Sonata' in *Three Classics in the Aesthetic of Music*, (New York, Dover, 1962; London, Marion Boyars, 1969)

'Memos', ed. J. Kirkpatrick (New York, W. W. Norton, 1972; London, Marion Boyars, 1973)

Mellers, W. *Music in a New-Found Land* (London, Barrie & Rockliff, 1964)

Perlis, V. (ed.) *Charles Ives Remembered, an Oral History* (New Haven, Yale University Press, 1974)

Rossiter, F. *Charles Ives and His America* (New York, Liveright, 1975)

Slonimsky, N. *Perfect Pitch* (New York, Oxford University Press, 1988)

Edgard Varèse

The definitive biography of Varèse awaits a visionary writer as yet unborn. Fernand Ouelette's *Edgard Varèse* and Louise Varèse's *Varèse, A Looking-Glass Diary*, Volume I, are journeyman efforts, with Louise's wifely, garrulous and factually flawed account ending at 1928. More valuable are the insights to be gleaned incidentally in the Rossiter, Mellers and Slonimsky entries under Ives (see above). Paul Griffiths's identical entries in the *New Grove Dictionary* and the *New Grove Dictionary of American Music* are also beyond reproach.

Bernard, J. W. *The Music of Edgard Varèse* (New Haven, Yale University Press, 1987)

Cowell, H. 'The Music of Edgard Varèse' in H. Cowell (ed.) *American Composers on American Music* (Stanford, Stanford University Press, 1933; revised Ungar Publishing, 1962)

Ouellette, F. *Edgard Varèse* (New York, Grossman, 1972; London, Marion Boyars, 1973)

Varèse, L. N. *A Looking-Glass Diary*, Vol. 1, 1883–1928 (New York, W. W. Norton, 1972)

Milton Babbitt

Babbitt, M. 'Who Cares if You Listen?' in E. Schwarz and B. Childs (ed.) *Contemporary Composers on Contemporary Music* (New York, Holt, Rinehart and Winston, 1967; New York, Da Capo, 1978)

Rockwell, J. 'The Northeastern Academic Establishment & the Romance of Science' in *All American Music* (New York, Alfred Knopf, 1983)

Earle Brown

Cage, J. *Silence* (Middletown, Connecticut, Wesleyan University Press, 1966; London, Marion Boyars, 1973)

La Barbara, J. 'Earle Brown's Homage to Alexander Calder' in *High Fidelity*, xxx 7, July 1980

Quist, P. L. *Indeterminate Form in the Works of Earle Brown* (diss), Baltimore, Peabody Conservatory of Music, 1984

George Crumb

Frank, A. 'George Crumb: Songs, Drones and Refrains of Death' in *(Music Library Association) Notes*, xxiii (1967)

Strickland, E. 'George Crumb' in *American Composers, Dialogues on Contemporary Music* (Bloomington, Indiana University Press, 1991)

Morton Feldman

Childs, B. 'Morton Feldman' in J, Vinton (ed.) *Dictionary of Contemporary Music* (New York, E.P. Dutton, 1971)

Dickinson, P. 'Feldman Explains Himself' in *Music and Musicians*, XIV/11, July 1966

Feldman, M. *Essays* (Cologne, Beginner Press, 1985)

Griffiths, P. 'Morton Feldman' in D. Arnold (ed.) *New Oxford Companion to Music* (London, Oxford University Press, 1983)

Lou Harrison

Rorem, N. 'Lou Harrison' in S. Sadie and W. Hitchcock (eds.) *New Grove Dictionary of American Music* (London and New York, Macmillan, 1986)

Schaefer, J. *New Sounds* (New York, Harper & Row, 1987)

Yates, P. 'Lou Harrison' in J. Vinton (ed.) *Dictionary of Contemporary Music* (New York, E.P. Dutton, 1971)

Luening/Ussachevsky

Schaefer, J. *New Sounds* (New York, Harper & Row, 1987)

Trimble, L. 'Otto Luening' and C. Wuorinen, 'Vladimir Ussachevsky' in S. Sadie and W. Hitchcock (eds.) *New Grove Dictionary of American Music* (London and New York, Macmillan, 1986)

Yates, P. *Twentieth-Century Music* (New York, Pantheon Press, 1967)

Colin McPhee

McPhee, C. *A House in Bali* (New York, Oxford University Press, 1946)

Oja, C.J. 'Colin McPhee, a Composer Turned Explorer' in *Tempo*. No. 148, 1984

Riegger, W. 'Adolph Weiss and Colin McPhee' in H. Cowell (ed.) *American Composers on American Music* (Stanford California, Stanford University Press, 1933, revised, Ungar Publishing, 1962)

Harry Partch

Augustine, D.S. *Four Theories of Music in the United States* (Ann Arbor, University of Michigan Press, 1979)

Bowen, M. 'Harry Partch' in *Music and Musicians* xiv/5, 1968

Partch, H. *Genesis of a Music* (New York, Da Capo, 1974)

Terry Riley

Griffiths, P. *Modern Music, the Avant-Garde Since 1945* (London, Dent; New York, Braziller, 1981)

Knox, K. 'The Parametric Music of Terry Riley' in *Jazz Monthly*, xiii/5, 1967

Kostelanetz, R. *On Innovative Musicians* (New York, Limelight, 1989)

Nyman, M. *Experimental Music, Cage and Beyond* (London, Macmillan, 1974)

Christian Wolff

Barry, M. 'Christian Wolff' in *Music and Musicians*, xxvi/7, 1978

Cage, J. *For the Birds* (London; Boston, Marion Boyars, 1981)

Nyman, M. 'Christian Wolff' in *Music and Musicians*, xx/8, 1972

La Monte Young

Griffiths, P. *Modern Music, the Avant-Garde Since 1945* (London, Dent; New York, Braziller, 1981)

Kostelanetz, R. *On Innovative Musicians* (New York, Limelight, 1989)

Nyman, M. *Experimental Music, Cage and Beyond* (New York, G. Schirmer, 1974)

Others

For information on the remaining pioneer experimenters considered here best sources are the articles in the *New Grove Dictionary of American Music* (four volumes) and John Vinton's *Dictionary of Contemporary Music* (New York, Dutton, 1975). John Schaefer's *New Sounds, A Listener's Guide to New Music* (New York, Harper & Row, 1987) is aimed at the casual listener, but contains some valid and enthusiastic insights on much of this music.

Gunn, K. *American Music in the Twentieth Century* (Belmont, California, Wadsworth/Thomson Learning, 1997)

Key, S. (ed) & Rothe, L. *American Mavericks* (Berkeley & Los Angeles, University of California Press, 2001)

Selective Discography

Milton Babbitt

Philomel/Phenomena
Judith Bettina (soprano); with Varèse's
Poème électronique
NEUMA 45074

Piano Works
Robert Taub
HARMONIA MUNDI 905160

Soli e Duettini
Various artists
BRIDGE 9135

Earle Brown

Much of Brown's music is written in a nontraditional
notation that allows the performer a certain control
over speed and texture. Two of his best-known works,
Available Forms I and II, allow the orchestral conductor
freedom to determine the sequence of events from large
independent blocks of music. Brown was also an eager
student of Viennese twelve-note music, especially the
music of Anton Webern, so that there is some overlap
between the freedoms he may have absorbed from Cage
and this Viennese discipline.

Corroboree, for three pianos
Degenhardt Piano Ensemble; with music by
George Crumb
MODE 19

Centering
San Francisco Contemporary Music Players
NEWPORT CLASSIC 85631

John Cage

Ask almost any ambitious composer, anywhere in the
world, to list the major influences on today's music,
and John Cage's name features near the top. One
reason is as simple as that question: 'why not?'
Whether the music Cage wrote leads to imitations is
less important than the sense of freedom he demanded,
both in music and in person, for every artist to make
unfettered decisions concerning creative responsibility.
He heartily disapproved of listening to music away
from the performance. 'Remove the records
from Texas', Cage once said, 'and someone will learn to
sing'. Cage did not like recordings; he liked his music
live; he liked it to be different every time, and he liked
active listeners.

By that standard, *4'33"* ought to be the work of
Cage best suited for recording, since the ambient
sounds are bound to change for every playing. As it
happens, there is a recording (in stereo), on
Hungaroton HC 12991, by the Hungarian percussion
group Amadinda, and another by Frank Zappa on the
splendid *A Chance Operation*, a tribute enlisting the
participation of New York's downtown scene almost in
its entirety, from Laurie Anderson to Zappa. Common
practice is to accord Cage the full value of his
iconoclastic pronouncements and to downgrade the
music itself as being of less importance. It is a theory
badly in need of re-examination. Here is a selection of
works for the open-minded to cherish:

A Chance Operation
Various artists; with tribute pieces by Christian Wolff,
David Tudor, James Tenney, Yoko Ono, etc.
KOCH INTERNATIONAL KIC 7238 (2 CDs)

Second and Third Constructions, for percussion quartet
New Music Consort; with music by Harrison,
Cowell, etc.
NEW WORLD 80405

Sonatas and Interludes for Prepared Piano
American Festival of Microtonal Music Ensemble; with
music by Ives
NEWPORT CLASSIC NPD 85526

Beyond their elegant, gamelan-like sounds, the dozens of pieces he wrote for prepared piano capture a side of Cage's own musical outlook that is rarely seen in later works: the simple, open, hypnotic antiqueness of the melodies, a clear descendant of Erik Satie's music (which Cage adored).

String Quartet in Four Parts
Four
Arditti Quartet
MODE 17, 27

Both works disarm the listener with their intense, simple quiet. *The String Quartet in Four Parts* instructs the players to perform without vibrato; this gives the music a kind of other-worldly character that matches the exotic effects from the prepared piano, revealing that even as traditional an ensemble as a string quartet can, with the right kind of urging, create a vocabulary of new sonorities, ravishing the ear and arousing the imagination. *Four*, the later of the two works, is arguably the most beautiful chamber-music composition of our time. Its players are each given a score for their single instrument; the confluences among the four occur largely by chance. Hearing this performance you may imagine that there is something more than sheer chance at work: a performing intuition that brings the music to juncture after juncture of harmonies so rich as to stop the breath.

Concert for Piano and Orchestra
Atlas Eclipticalis
Orchestra of S. E. M. conducted by Petr Kotik
WERGO 6216-2

Here is Cage for the strong of heart: tense, explosive, tough pieces whose ultimate shape is achieved through non-traditional means. The *Concert* has no overall score; it exists as a series of single scores for the pianist (who could, actually, go it alone) and for a group of solo instruments which overlay the piano part without interlocking. *Atlas Eclipticalis* is, as its name describes, a star-map: a work whose notes are derived from laying transparencies of celestial charts over lined music paper and, thus, change with the day. The music survives on the strength of its punching energy and sheer nerve.

Indeterminacy
John Cage, speaker, with David Tudor, pianist
SMITHSONIAN- FOLKWAYS 40804/5

John Cage reads, in his seductively buttery, if slightly twee delivery, ninety tiny anecdotes or mood pieces, each lasting exactly a minute, while – as if in the next room with the door ajar – pianist David Tudor provides discreet punctuation.

Quartets
Music for 14
San Francisco Contemporary Music Players conducted by Steven Mosko
NEWPORT CLASSIC 85547

Never one to reject his American-iconoclast heritage, Cage in the *Quartets* has taken eight hymns by Revolutionary-era New England composers, fragmented them and woven them into a new musical fabric. A large orchestra is used, but only four players perform at any one time. The sound is like a nocturnal landscape, with several church suppers and singing going on in the distance, with the listener in the foreground absorbing the enchanting blend. If this sounds rather like Charles Ives, perhaps it is, and beautiful of its kind.

There is no notated score for *Music for 14*; the parts are 'to be played as if from six centres in space'. And what of us listeners, marooned out there in one or another block of Cageian space? Hearing his music on a recording, the same every time repeated, defeats some part of Cage's notion of constant change, constant autonomy. Yet, it could be that many of Cage's fervent admirers, as well as his most outspoken detractors, miss an important aspect of his indeterminate music: its beauty. Bright, irregular splotches of colour rush by; think a rush of butterflies, a Calder mobile, a Pollock canvas, why not? Cage was a master of all the arts, all the senses, and in these two extended works they are all happily put on display.

Europera 5
Vocal ensemble, with Yvar Mikhashoff (piano)
MODE 36

Freeman Études
Irvine Arditti (violin)
MODE 32

A recording at virtuoso speeds that astonished and
delighted the composer.

Henry Cowell

Considering the size of his output, Cowell is not well
represented on record. Two recordings from the 1990s
went some way to amend that situation: a miscellany of
chamber works conducted by Richard Auldon Clark on
Koch International, and a reissue of Cowell's 1958
recordings of piano works on Smithsonian/Folkways.
Cowell's fate seems to be as a makeweight to the music
of others (who, in some cases, might well owe him their
existence). Of these, the New Albion disc by the
Abel–Steinberg–Winant Trio, which includes the *Set of
Five* along with interesting works by Cage and
Harrison, is by far the most attractive.

Cowell Piano Music
Henry Cowell (piano); recorded in 1958, with Cowell's
commentary
SMITHSONIAN-FOLKWAYS 40801

Music of Cowell
Manhattan Chamber Orchestra conducted by
R.A. Clark (including *Melting Pot* for orchestra,
Persian Set, Hymn and Fuguing Tune, etc.)
KOCH INTERNATIONAL KIC 7220

Set of Five
Abel–Steinberg–Winant Trio; with music by Cage,
Harrison and Hovhaness
NEW ALBION 036

Quartet Euphometric
Emerson Quartet; with music by Imbrie, Schuller
NEW WORLD 80453

George Crumb

Ancient Voices of Children
Jan DeGaetani with an ensemble conducted by Arthur
Weisberg
ELEKTRA-NONESUCH 79149-2

Black Angels
Kronos Quartet
ELEKTRA-NONESUCH 79242-2

Star Child
Warsaw Philharmonic, Thomas Conlon
BRIDGE 9095

Morton Feldman

The flamboyant Morton Feldman cut an intriguing if
controversial figure, with his bluff, larger-than-life
persona that masked a profound musical wisdom.
Nurtured in the academic atonality, Feldman
encountered his cultural epiphany around 1950 with
his discovery of John Cage's dogma that a work of
music can be anything its composer says it is. Under
Cage's influence Feldman developed his own formula
for attaining artistic freedom. He developed a graphic
notation that allowed the performer considerable
freedom of choice – of rhythm, pitch and dynamics.
He wrote for the most part for small ensemble, and his
music is often marked by an intense quietude: a kind
of still, grey continuum filled with points of colour,
and often running on for several hours. He was little
interested in electronics; one or two pieces convinced
him that traditional instruments were here to stay, for a
while at least.

For Samuel Beckett
San Francisco Contemporary Music Players, conducted
by Steven Mosko
NEWPORT CLASSIC 85506

Lou Harrison

Lou Harrison has been more lavishly treated, with several of his works – including the spellbinding *Lo Koro Sutro* for chorus (singing in Esperanto) and gamelan, and an early work of considerable power, *The Perilous Chapel* of 1948 – on the San Francisco label New Albion, and the Piano Concerto (played by Keith Jarrett, for whom it was written) on New World Records, coupled with the immensely charming Suite from 1961, scored for traditional Western instruments but with sections that imitate the sounds of gamelan.

Piano Concerto
Keith Jarrett (piano); New Japan Philharmonic
NEW WORLD 366-2

Lo Koro Sutro
University of California Chorus
NEW ALBION NA 015

Charles Ives

After nearly a half-century of silence, Ives's music made its triumphant entry into the record catalogues early in the LP era. Multiple recordings exist of most of the major orchestral works, with the majority of the successful recordings managed by American hands: the conductors Leonard Bernstein, Michael Tilson Thomas and Leonard Slatkin; the pianist Gilbert Kalish and the great, late singer Jan DeGaetani. There have been, of course, invaders from abroad; Sir Neville Marriner and his Academy of St. Martin-in-the-Fields contribute a creditable Third Symphony. The chances are, however, that the resolutely chauvinistic Ives would not approve.

Central Park in the Dark
'Holidays' Symphony
The Unanswered Question
Chicago Symphony Orchestra conducted by
Michael Tilson Thomas
SONY MK 42381

Symphonies Nos. 1 and 4
Chicago Symphony Orchestra conducted by Michael Tilson Thomas; includes choral performances of the hymns used in the Fourth Symphony
SONY SK 44939

Symphonies Nos. 2 and 3
New York Philharmonic Orchestra conducted by
Leonard Bernstein
SONY SMK 47568

Three Places in New England
St Louis Symphony Orchestra conducted by
Leonard Slatkin
RCA 09026-61222-2

'Concord' Sonata
Gilbert Kalish (piano)
ELEKTRA-NONESUCH 71337-2

'Concord' Sonata
Easley Blackwood (piano)
CEDILLE 90000 005

String Quartets Nos. 1 and 2
Emerson Quartet
DEUTSCHE GRAMMOPHON 435864-2

Songs
Jan DeGaetani (soprano)
ELEKTRA-NONESUCH 71325-2

Songs
Thomas Hampson (baritone)
TELDEC 9031-72168

They Are There
Charles Ives's 1942 recording, singing his own song with piano accompaniment, is surrounded by the sound of the Kronos Quartet in a kind of collage
ELEKTRA-NONESUCH 79242-2

Otto Luening & Vladimir Ussachevsky

The Luening-Ussachevsky *Incantation for Electronic Tape*, one of their first collaborations, is part of the 'Pioneers of Electronic Music' collection (NEW WORLD 80644).

Colin McPhee

For all the work's fame as a transcultural musical phenomenon, the first recording of McPhee's *Tabuh-tabuhan* from 1956 was the only version available for many years:

Tabuh-tabuhan
Eastman- Rochester Symphony Orchestra conducted by Howard Hanson; with works by Roger Sessions and Virgil Thomson
PHILIPS-MERCURY 434310-2

Harry Partch

Most of the available Harry Partch consists of performances he led in the 1960s, sometimes recorded at live performances and, therefore, rather faded in sound. The one thoroughly modern Partch recording is the two-disc set of *Revelation in the Courthouse Park* on the Tomato label, with the wonderful sounds of Partch's instruments against a rather feeble marching band and an amateurish mouthing of the text.

The Bewitched
University of Illinois Ensemble
CRI 7001

Revelation in the Courthouse Park
Ensemble conducted by Danlee Mitchell
TOMATO RZ-70390

The Delusion of the Fury
Ensemble conducted by Danlee Mitchell
INNOVA 406

Terry Riley

Terry Riley's *In C* has had several recordings, of which the one by the Shanghai Film Orchestra, on the aptly-named Celestial Harmonies label, deserves your undying affection.

In C
University of Buffalo players
SONY MK 07178

In C
Shanghai Film Orchestra
CELESTIAL HARMONIES 13062-2

Cadenza on the Night Plain
Kronos Quartet
GRAMAVISION R22Z 79444-2 (2 CDs)

Salome Dances for Peace
Kronos Quartet
NONESUCH 79217 (2 CDs)

Shri Camel
Terry Riley; with other works for electronic organ
SONY CLASSICAL 35164

Edgard Varèse

All twelve of Varèse's acknowledged works have been satisfactorily recorded. His principal interpreters are Boulez, whose marvellous sense of control draws immaculate and spirited performances from his Paris-based Ensemble InterContemporain on several Sony discs; the late Maurice Abravanel, whose distinguished Vanguard recordings with the Utah Symphony Orchestra include a version of the unfinished *Nocturnal*; and Arthur Weisberg, whose single Nonesuch disc includes a radiant performance of *Offrandes* by the late Jan DeGaetani.

Nocturnal
Amériques
Utah Symphony Orchestra conducted by Maurice
Abravanel with Ariel Bybee (soprano); with Honegger's
Pacific 231
VANGUARD CLASSICS OVC 7031

Déserts
Intégrales
Ionisation
Poème électronique
ASKO Ensemble
ATTACCA-BABEL 9263-2

Amériques
Arcana
Density 21.5
Intégrales
Ionisation
New York Philharmonic and the Ensemble
InterContemporain conducted by Pierre Boulez
SONY SK 45844

Ecuatorial
Intégrales
Octandre
Offrandes
Contemporary Chamber Ensemble conducted by
Arthur Weisberg with Jan DeGaetani (soprano)
NONESUCH 71269

La Monte Young

The Well-Tuned Piano
La Monte Young (piano)
GRAMAVISION R255 76945-2

Christian Wolff

Mayday Materials
Christian Wolff (synclavier) and ensemble; with works
by Appleton, Jones
CENTAUR 2052

Index

Page numbers in italics refer to
picture captions.

**Photographic
Acknowledgements**